W9-DBH-140

RENAISSANCE

VOLUME 3

Copernicus — Exploration

GROLIER
EDUCATIONAL

Published by Grolier Educational
Sherman Turnpike
Danbury, Connecticut 06816

Set ISBN 0-7172-5673-1
Volume 3 ISBN 0-7172-5665-0

Library of Congress Cataloging-in-Publication Data

Renaissance.
    p. cm.
Summary: Chronicles the cultural and artistic flowering
known as the Renaissance that flourished in Europe and
in other parts of the world from approximately 1375 to
1575 A.D.
Includes index.
Contents: v. 1. Africa–Bologna — v. 2. Books and libraries–
Constantinople — v. 3. Copernicus–Exploration — v. 4.
Eyck–Government — v. 5. Guilds and crafts–Landscape
painting — v. 6. Language–Merchants — v. 7. Michelangelo–
Palaces and villas — v. 8. Palestrina–Reformation — v. 9.
Religious dissent–Tapestry — v. 10. Technology–Zwingli.
    ISBN 0-7172-5673-1 (set : alk. paper)
    1. Renaissance—Juvenile literature. [1. Renaissance.]
I. Grolier Educational (Firm)
  CB361 .R367 2002
  940.2'1—dc21
                      2002002477

For information address the publisher:
Grolier Educational, Sherman Turnpike,
Danbury, Connecticut 06816

FOR BROWN PARTWORKS

Project Editor: Shona Grimbly
Deputy Editor: Rachel Bean
Text Editor: Chris King
Designer: Sarah Williams
Picture Research: Veneta Bullen
Maps: Colin Woodman
Design Manager: Lynne Ross
Production: Matt Weyland
Managing Editor: Tim Cooke
Consultant: Stephen A. McKnight
                         University of Florida

Printed and bound in Singapore

ABOUT THIS BOOK

This is one of a set of 10 books that tells the story of the Renaissance—a time of discovery and change in the world. It was during this period—roughly from 1375 to 1575—that adventurous mariners from Europe sailed the vast oceans in tiny ships and found the Americas and new sea routes to the Spice Islands of the East. The influx of gold and silver from the New World and the increase in trade made many merchants and traders in Europe extremely rich. They spent some of their wealth on luxury goods like paintings and gold and silver items for their homes, and this created a new demand for the work of artists of all kinds. Europe experienced a cultural flowering as great artists like Leonardo da Vinci, Michelangelo, and Raphael produced masterpieces that have never been surpassed.

At the same time, scholars were rediscovering the works of the ancient Greek and Roman writers, and this led to a new way of looking at the world based on observation and the importance of the individual. This humanism, together with other new ideas, spread more rapidly than ever before thanks to the development of printing with movable type.

There was upheaval in the church too. Thinkers such as Erasmus and Luther began to question the teachings of the established church, and this eventually led to a breakaway from the Catholic church and the setting up of Protestant churches—an event called the Reformation.

The set focuses on Europe, but it also looks at how societies in other parts of the world such as Africa, China, India, and the Americas were developing, and the ways in which the Islamic and Christian worlds interacted.

The entries in this set are arranged alphabetically and are illustrated with paintings, photographs, drawings, and maps, many from the Renaissance period. Each entry ends with a list of cross-references to other entries in the set, and at the end of each book there is a timeline to help you relate events to one another in time.

There is also a useful "Further Reading" list that includes websites, a glossary of special terms, and an index covering the whole set.

Contents

Copernicus

The Polish astronomer Nicolaus Copernicus (1473–1543) is remembered for developing the theory that the earth and other planets move around the sun. Up until that time people had believed that the sun and the planets moved around the earth, which was stationary at the center of the universe. Copernicus's theory began a revolution in astronomy that was to influence the whole course of modern science.

Copernicus was born in Torun, a town on the Vistula River in central Poland. He was named Mikolaj Kopernik in Polish, but he was later known by the Latin version of his name that we use today. His father was a prosperous merchant; and after he died, the young

His studies were leading to a revolutionary conclusion

Copernicus was brought up by an uncle who became bishop of Ermeland. In 1491, at the age of 18, Copernicus went to study at the University of Krakow, which was famous for its teachings in astronomy, mathematics, and philosophy. In 1496 he traveled to Italy and over the next few years he studied church law, Greek philosophy, and medicine at Bologna, Padua, and Ferrara.

On his return to Poland Copernicus became a canon, or church official, at the cathedral of Frombork. His duties

left him plenty of time to continue his studies of the stars. He was particularly interested in the supposed orbits of the sun, moon, and planets around the earth, which was then thought to be the very center of the universe.

In 1514 Copernicus was asked by the pope to look at ways of reforming the calendar that had been in use since the days of Julius Caesar and was now severely out of line with the seasons. He decided, however, that there was not enough accurate information on the positions and movements of the sun and moon to correct the calendar. To get better information Copernicus undertook further studies that led him to a revolutionary conclusion.

According to the ancient Greek astronomer Ptolemy, the earth was fixed at the center of the universe, while all the stars and planets traveled

Above: An astrological map of the heavens dating from about 1543, drawn according to the Copernican system. It shows the earth, planets, and the zodiac circling the sun, which is at the center.

Below: A statue of Copernicus in Montreal, Canada. Copernicus's revolutionary view of the planetary system met with opposition from religious leaders.

around it in complicated patterns. Ptolemy's view was universally accepted at that time. Copernicus, however, became more and more convinced that Ptolemy was wrong.

Copernicus concluded—rightly—that the earth turned on its axis once every day as it went on a yearly orbit around the sun. This accounted for the apparent movements of the sun and stars. It was a much simpler explanation than that put forward by Ptolemy and was similar to theories developed before Ptolemy's time by the Greek astronomer Aristarchus of Samos.

Copernicus, however, did not rush to publish his ideas. The church—as well as other scholars—believed firmly in the Ptolemaic system. As a church official and a Christian, Copernicus had no wish to quarrel with the pope.

Nevertheless, Copernicus went on making mathematical calculations and drawing diagrams to back up his theories. He showed them to

friends and other scholars, who urged him to make them known more widely. By 1540 his original ideas had grown into a six-part work entitled *The Revolutions of the Heavenly Spheres*. A supporter named Georg Joachim Rheticus took the manuscript to be printed in Nuremberg, in Protestant Germany, where it was thought there might be less hostility to Copernicus's ideas than in Catholic Poland. But the new theories met with opposition from Martin Luther and other religious leaders. Finally, the book was printed in Leipzig in 1543.

TRANSFORMING THE UNIVERSE

Copernicus died in the year his book was published. It outraged many people because it directly contradicted the teachings of the church. His ideas transformed the way we look at the universe and also paved the way for important discoveries in the following years by such great scientists as Brahe, Kepler, and Galileo.

SEE ALSO

♦ Astronomy
♦ Calendars and
  Clocks
♦ Galileo
♦ Luther

Correggio

Correggio (about 1489–1534) was an Italian artist famous for his dramatic paintings decorating the domed ceilings of churches. He made these domes look as if they were open to the heavens by painting brilliant light flooding in from between sunlit clouds. Against this background he depicted holy figures as if seen from below, an effect he achieved by foreshortening, or compressing, the proportions of their bodies. These dramatic, light-filled paintings created a startling effect in the dark churches they adorned.

Correggio's real name was Antonio Allegri. He named himself after the small Italian city of Correggio where he was born. He first learned painting from his uncle, who was an artist, before studying in Modena and Mantua. Correggio was influenced by the early Renaissance painter Andrea Mantegna and also by Leonardo da Vinci, Raphael, and Michelangelo.

Above: A detail of Correggio's huge painting The Assumption of the Virgin *(about 1526) on the dome of Parma Cathedral. Correggio painted the Virgin as she had never been shown before, with her legs dangling down as she rises up to heaven.*

SEE ALSO

♦ Baroque
♦ Leonardo da Vinci
♦ Mantegna
♦ Michelangelo
♦ Painting
♦ Perspective
♦ Raphael

Correggio produced his greatest works in the decade 1520 to 1530. They are two huge frescoes (paintings made on wet plaster) on the domes of the church of San Giovanni Evangelista in Parma and Parma Cathedral. Both are illusionistic, or trompe l'oeil, a French term that means "tricking the eye." They are painted to look as if there is no dome, and the church is open to the sky. The holy figures are depicted as if seen from below, many with their legs dangling downward. The effect is very dramatic, but some people objected because they thought it was an undignified way to show holy figures. The subject of the painting in San Giovanni Evangelista is the Ascension of Christ, when Christ rose from earth to heaven, and in the cathedral, the Assumption of the Virgin, when Mary was taken up to heaven.

ALTARPIECES AND OTHER WORKS

As well as these ceilings Correggio also produced several large paintings to go behind altars, including *The Holy Night* (about 1530). This picture shows Mary and Joseph with the newly born Jesus in a stable and uses the same brilliant light effects as his ceilings. Correggio also painted subjects from classical (ancient Greek and Roman) myths, including a series called *The Loves of Jupiter*, in which he depicted the female body with great skill and delicacy.

Correggio died in 1534, aged about 45. The pioneering techniques he used in his dome frescoes were taken up by later artists working in the baroque style that dominated European art in the 17th and 18th centuries.

Counter Reformation

The Counter Reformation was a religious movement that took place within the Catholic church from the early 16th century onward. It centered around attempts by the church to renew and strengthen itself, mainly in response to the threat posed by Protestantism.

Above: A portrait of Pope Paul III by the Venetian artist Titian. Paul presided over the Council of Trent and is often described as the first pope of the Counter Reformation.

At the start of the 16th century many people felt that the church had become corrupt. Critics believed that many church officials and priests used their status to build up their own personal wealth and spent too much of their time involved in politics. The climax to this growing feeling of resentment came in 1517, when the German monk Martin Luther (1483–1546) pinned 95 theses, or articles, to the church door in Wittenburg. Luther's theses not only attacked clerical abuses, but also challenged many official church beliefs. His teachings quickly became popular and soon formed the basis of a new branch of Christianity—Protestantism. This religious revolution is known as the Reformation.

GROWTH OF PROTESTANTISM

Protestantism spread very quickly, especially in northern Europe. Even before Luther many clerics had recognized the problems facing the church and tried to address them from within. However, the rapid growth of Protestantism provided a huge incentive for the church to reform itself. The first real steps in the Counter Reformation were taken during the papacy of Paul III (pope 1534–1546), when the church actively responded to the threat of Protestantism.

One of the first of these measures was the establishment of a reform commission in 1536. The commission's job was to report back to the pope on the state of the church. Its findings echoed many of the criticisms that the Protestants had been making. It found that corruption was widespread and that there were abuses in the sale of indulgences—certificates that promised to reduce the amount of time that people's souls suffered in purgatory to atone for their sins.

In 1542 a far harsher way of fighting Protestantism arrived when the Roman Inquisition was established. It was simply a revival of a medieval means of

Right: Church leaders in discussion at the Council of Trent. The council was a key event in the history of the Catholic church. Many of the church's basic doctrines were defined there.

stamping out heresy, or beliefs that ran contrary to those of the Catholic church. The Inquisition used brutal methods against the church's enemies—torture was used to extract confessions, while heretics who refused to recant their beliefs were often executed.

THE COUNCIL OF TRENT

If heresy was to be combated, then it was important that the official beliefs or doctrines of the church were properly defined. The need for such definitions was one of the reasons why Pope Paul III organized the Council of Trent. A council was an assembly where church leaders discussed and ruled on issues of doctrine. Often popes had been unwilling to call councils since they saw them as threats to their own authority. However, Paul knew that a council was necessary if the church was to be reformed effectively.

The council first met in the Italian town of Trent in December 1545 and did not conclude until 1563. It was split into three separate sessions—the first lasted from 1545 to 1547, the second from 1551 to 1552, and the third from 1562 to 1563. The council was made up of clerics from all over Europe.

The council made a great number of decisions that drew a clear line between Catholicism and Protestantism. Among the most important was the belief that people achieved salvation through a combination of faith in God and good works, rather than by faith alone, as Protestants believed. The council reaffirmed the doctrine of transubstantiation, the belief that the bread and wine used in the ritual of Communion literally become the body and blood of Christ. It also confirmed the existence of purgatory and ruled that the Latin Vulgate Bible was the only authentic version—Protestants encouraged the translation of the scriptures into local languages.

As well as ruling on theoretical issues, the Council of Trent also addressed some of the abuses and corruption that existed within the church. It condemned the sale of indulgences for profit and the practice of bishops living away from their dioceses, or areas under their control. It gave the pope increased authority over the church and also forced female religious orders to live in enclosed communities. Overall, the Council of Trent clarified the distinction between Catholicism and Protestantism, and reinforced the moral authority of church officials by correcting the most obvious abuses. A stronger and more energetic church emerged, ready to inspire its members and to win back many of those lost to Protestantism.

The fight against Protestantism was spearheaded by a group known as the Jesuits. The Jesuit order was founded by the Spanish nobleman Ignatius de Loyola in 1540. It was only one of many new religious orders that sprang up in the first half of the 16th century. Others included the Ursulines, an all-female order, and the Capuchins, a stricter branch of the existing Franciscans. Groups such as these tried to re-invigorate the church by living a pure and simple life and returning to the spirit of Christ's teachings.

RISE OF THE JESUITS

The Jesuits quickly grew to overshadow the other groups both in size and in importance. Their success was the result of their high levels of training, discipline, and military-style organization, combined with the fact that Loyola only recruited men of outstanding intellectual ability. More than any other order, the energetic Jesuits set out to travel the world, spreading the Catholic faith and attacking Protestantism. They placed a great emphasis on education and founded many schools, which helped increase their influence. By the end of

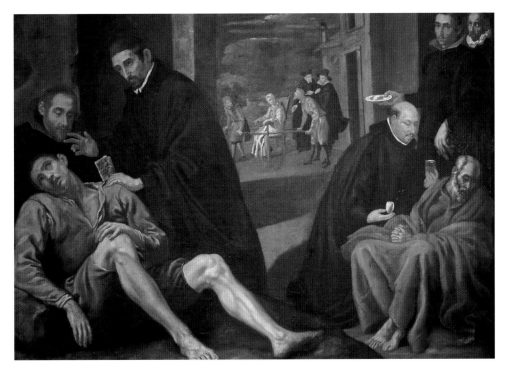

Left: A painting of Jesuit monks caring for the poor. The Jesuits were responsible for spreading the Catholic faith to new areas of the world. They also tried to halt the growth of Protestantism in northern Europe.

THE INDEX OF FORBIDDEN BOOKS

The invention of the printing press in the mid-15th century made it far easier for heretical or revolutionary thinkers to spread their ideas. In response the Catholic church began to publish lists of works that met with its disapproval. The first Index of Prohibited Books was published by Pope Paul IV in 1559. It included not only works by Protestant thinkers, but also books and poems by literary figures such as Dante, Machiavelli, and Erasmus.

The Council of Trent later published a revised list, which is estimated to have covered nearly three-quarters of all books that were being printed in Europe at the time. Pope Pius IV also appointed a group of clerics known as the Congregation of the Index to continually update the list. New versions of the index were published until 1948.

Right: Dominican monks working as inquisitors burn forbidden books. Book burning was one way in which the church combated hostile ideas.

the 16th century Jesuits had traveled to Africa, China, Japan, and the Americas, gaining thousands of new converts to Catholicism in the process. They had also halted the spread of Protestantism in many parts of northern Europe.

THE CATHOLIC REVIVAL

The revival of Catholicism was also the result of the efforts of the popes who ruled in the second half of the 16th century. Many of the men who held the papacy in the 15th century led lives like Renaissance princes. The popes of the 16th century, however, were far more concerned with spiritual matters. Paul IV (pope 1555–1559) and Pius V (pope 1566–1572) were both fiercely committed to the battle against heresy and pursued vigorous campaigns against Protestantism. Their immediate successors, Gregory XIII (pope 1572–

1585) and Sixtus V (pope 1585–1590), strengthened the church by promoting religious education and reorganizing its administration respectively.

By 1600 the Counter Reformation had successfully halted the advance of Protestantism, and by 1660 it had won back much of the territory previously lost. Although reformed churches were successfully established in many parts of northern Europe, including Scandinavia, Scotland, England, the Netherlands, and most of Germany, Catholicism had been restored to Poland, southern Germany, Hungary, Austria, Bohemia, and much of France. In southern European countries such as Spain and Italy the threat of Protestantism had been almost completely wiped out. In many ways the Catholic church was stronger than it had been for centuries.

Courts and Court Culture

During the Renaissance the courts of the nobility and royalty played a crucial role in the development of art and politics. Whether they were in small city-states or large kingdoms, rulers' courts performed several key functions. They housed the ruler's personal household, were the focus of government administration and politics, and became centers of art and literature. Courts were also places where rulers displayed their power and wealth through lavish festivities.

All important rulers had courts, whether they were emperors, kings, dukes, or popes. Courts followed rulers

Below: This 16th-century painting shows a ball at the French royal court. The courtiers wear fashionable clothes and dance to music played by a group of musicians.

when they traveled but were generally based in a castle or palace in the capital city. The number of people who lived at court varied, but larger courts often housed more than a thousand people. As well as the ruler and the ruler's family, they included nobles, foreign diplomats, artists, servants, household and government officials, scholars, jesters, court ladies, and noble children.

In the Renaissance courts weren't just presided over by men. There were a growing number of women rulers during this period, from Catherine de Médicis in France to Queen Elizabeth I in England. The status of female courtiers also increased. They were often highly educated and valued members of court, although they were still not considered the equal of their male counterparts.

COURTLY LIFE AND BEHAVIOR

Besides the ruler, the most important members of a court were the nobles. As the ruler centralized power, courts grew, and the nobility were increasingly compelled to live there to serve their ruler in return for rewards, such as titles, pensions, or gifts of land. Although life at court seemed splendid and exciting to outsiders, for the courtier it was often tedious. They also lived in a state of constant tension and competitiveness as they attempted to advance themselves over other courtiers by pleasing the ruler.

One of the ways courtiers tried to gain their ruler's favor was by following strict rules of polite behavior, or etiquette. Manners came to play an

CASTIGLIONE'S COURTIER

The Courtier was written by the Italian humanist and poet Baldassare Castiglione (1478–1529), a diplomat who served at the court of the duke of Urbino. The book describes the perfect courtier and draws a vivid portrait of Renaissance court society. It was published in 1528 and was translated and copied many times. The book is set out as a conversation between courtiers and ladies in the court at Urbino. They discuss the ideal courtier and decide that he should be aristocratic, athletic, learned, and skilled in the arts. He should also be charming and well-mannered, control his emotions and behavior, and speak with grace. This view of courtly behavior combined medieval traditions of chivalry with new humanist ideas on the "universal man," a man who excelled in all areas of life and culture.

Above: A portrait of Castiglione painted in about 1514 by his friend Raphael, who grew up in the court at Urbino.

important part in court life in the Renaissance, as is indicated by the word "courtesy," which comes from the word "court." Many treatises (books) were written on the subject, the most famous of which is *The Courtier* by Baldassare Castiglione (see box).

DISPLAYS OF POWER AND WEALTH

In addition to being the centers of government, courts were also places to display the ruler's wealth and authority. They were housed in impressive castles and palaces with huge defensive walls, towers, and battlements that were clear symbols of power. Inside there were private rooms for the ruler and the ruler's family and public rooms for government business. Artists were employed to decorate these rooms with carvings, tapestries, and paintings, and to design costumes, banners, and scenery for lavish festivities held there.

Court festivals were extravagant affairs intended to entertain courtiers and impress visitors. The celebrations often lasted days and featured banquets, parades, theater and music, dances, and tournaments.

Renaissance rulers also displayed their superiority through learning and culture. They employed leading artists, writers, and musicians, and hired humanist scholars to educate their children and act as advisers.

Some of the wealthiest and most powerful courts in the 15th and 16th centuries were those belonging to dukes in Burgundy, Milan, Florence, and Mantua, to the pope in Rome, and to King Francis I in France and the Tudor monarchs in England. They all influenced smaller courts and set trends in fashions, etiquette, and the arts that influenced European court life for centuries to come.

SEE ALSO
♦ Elizabeth I
♦ Este Family
♦ Francis I
♦ Gonzaga Family
♦ Government, Systems of
♦ Humanism
♦ Patronage
♦ Sforza Family

Crime and Punishment

The Renaissance was an age when a large number of people lived on the edges of the community. Frequently they were forced into crime. Landless laborers, immigrants seeking work, men and women driven from their villages by hunger or disease, orphans, and widows formed a floating population. They moved from place to place, seeking work or charity, and sometimes preying on those who were richer, and luckier, than themselves. Those who did resort to crime were taking terrible risks. Penalties for criminals were extremely harsh.

Towns were centers of criminal activity, magnets for outcasts and the poor. Gangs of pickpockets often operated on the city streets. They were called "cutpurses" since they cut away the purses that people carried tied to their waists. Many urban beggars were organized into criminal gangs. They specialized in various types of deceit. A teenage beggar arrested in Rome in 1595 testified that the beggars of the city were grouped into fellowships, each specializing in a different activity. Their crimes ranged from faking illness to purse-snatching.

The countryside could also be dangerous, and people who had to travel along lonely country roads did so in daylight in large groups. They were very careful to conceal their money. Travelers were often scared by tales of criminal gangs, who were said to roam the countryside looking for victims. Although these stories exaggerated the dangers of travel, such gangs did exist. They could range greatly in size from a handful of ragged adolescents to extremely large, well-organized, and well-armed groups of men.

Left: This 16th-century German woodcut shows robbers dividing their booty after ambushing a party of merchants. City dwellers imagined the forests and countryside to be full of roaming bands of criminals.

Official records of people convicted of crime in the 14th and 15th centuries suggest that almost all offenders were poor vagrants. However, the rich were also responsible for many crimes, ranging from robbery to extortion. Powerful noblemen were unlikely to be tried for their crimes, and their actions usually went unpunished.

PUNISHMENT

The fight against crime was haphazard. City wards elected and provided their own constables, who were responsible for keeping order and pursuing criminals. Once criminals were caught, they were held in jail only until sentence was passed.

Because they were designed to act as a deterrent, punishments were very harsh. They were generally carried out in public, since they were intended to be a warning to others. Theft, the most common crime, was subject to a range of penalties, from hanging to branding with a hot iron.

Even petty criminals were very harshly punished. For example, a dishonest tradesman might be sentenced to three days in the stocks—two wooden planks that secured his feet—or the pillory, a wooden board that secured his head and arms. Put on public display, criminals were then further humiliated—angry victims were encouraged to pelt them with rotten vegetables.

The most popular spectacles of all were executions. Townspeople enjoyed following the solemn procession to the execution ground and cheered when the hanged man swung from the gibbet. In some cases death by hanging alone was not considered harsh enough. Traitors were hanged, drawn, and quartered. This meant that they were hanged, cut down while still alive,

disemboweled, and then their bodies were cut into four pieces. Other common means of execution included beheading and burning at the stake.

HERESY

Heretics were people whose religious beliefs contradicted the teachings of the church. They were often persecuted by the church authorities, who used torture to extract confessions of heretical beliefs from their prisoners. Once the confessions had been secured, the prisoners were subject to an auto-da-fé (act of faith), in which they were paraded through the streets and then publicly sentenced. Frequently they were burned at the stake.

Above: This woodcut shows some of the many gruesome punishments that could await criminals during the Renaissance.

SEE ALSO
♦ Inquisition
♦ Justice and the Law
♦ Poverty
♦ Violence

Daily Life

Renaissance Europe was mainly rural, with 75 percent of the population living directly off the land. For the vast majority life was hard. Many people scraped a living from farming and were vulnerable to disease, famine, or poor harvests. Wealth was concentrated in the hands of a few landowners, although towns were also vibrant economic centers where rich merchants and bankers enjoyed luxurious lifestyles.

In the countryside life was dominated by work. Peasants rose at sunrise, winter and summer, and spent their days tending their fields and livestock. Children helped with these tasks from an early age. Women were responsible for the household. They prepared and cooked food, carried water from the communal well or stream, cleaned, washed, spun wool, and wove basic cloth to make their family's clothes. Women were also expected to help in the fields with planting and harvesting.

This hard existence took its toll on health. Country people were stunted in their growth, had poor teeth, swollen bellies, and many skin diseases caused by malnutrition. On average, one in four babies died in the first year of their

Below: This picture by Pieter Bruegel the Elder shows haymaking and other summertime activities. Peasants cut and gather hay, and load it onto a wagon. They also carry freshly harvested fruit and vegetables back to their village.

Above: An early 17th-century painting of villagers slaughtering and butchering pigs. Some meat was eaten right away, and the rest was salted or hung in the smoke of household fires to preserve it.

lives, and many more children died before reaching adulthood. Poor hygiene and healthcare also meant that many women died in childbirth.

Living conditions were primitive. The vast majority of peasants lived in windowless houses of only one or two rooms. They had an attic in which food was stored in the winter, plus a barn and a cowshed. The houses were overrun with rats, fleas, and lice, and they were also smelly and smoky. People rarely took baths, and the latrines, or toilets, were little more than foul-smelling pits dug in the backyard. Wood fires filled the poorly ventilated rooms with smoke. If wood was in short supply, conditions in winter were bitterly cold. After dark people relied on firelight or, if they could afford them, candles or oil lamps for light; but most country dwellers went to bed early, especially in the wintertime.

Bread and grain such as wheat, rye, oats, and millet dominated the diet. A typical peasant meal consisted of a hunk of bread served with a thin soup of vegetables. Meat was a rare treat and when it was eaten was usually pork. The peasant diet in general was lacking in fresh fruit and vegetables. The fresh produce of summer and autumn was preserved in order to last people through the winter—pork was salted or cured over the hearth, and vegetables and fruit were pickled.

MONEY BUYS COMFORT

Some villagers had more comfortable lives. Yeomen, or tenant farmers, leased their land from the lord of the manor and owned a team of horses and a plow. They had the means to produce a surplus of food, which they sold. Money enabled them to buy a few luxuries such as extra clothes and household linen, a feather mattress, and solid wooden furniture. The village miller, who ground all the local grain, and the blacksmith provided essential services and also had more comfortable lives than most villagers. People bought any other goods they needed from peddlers who wandered from place to place selling items of clothing, ribbons, and trinkets.

Sunday was the day of rest, when people attended their local church. Leisure time was normally restricted to the local inn, where groups of traveling "players," or actors, sometimes performed. People looked forward eagerly to market days, when they took their produce to the local town, as well as to holidays and festivals, when the monotony of daily life was relieved by feasting and celebrations.

For most town dwellers life was also dominated by work, although there were many more distractions. Craftsmen lived in dark, narrow-fronted houses with their workshops on the first floor and their living quarters on the second and third floors above. They were members of guilds, organizations set up to regulate crafts and professions, and their social lives revolved around other guild members, processions, and banquets.

ROUTINES OF TOWN LIFE

The working day began early. Church bells rang at 4:00 A.M. signifying the end of the curfew, when people were not allowed out on the streets. The gates to the cities were thrown open, and another day began. Jobbing laborers, such as carpenters and

FEASTS AND FESTIVALS

In the countryside people looked forward with enthusiasm to saints' days and to the major festivals of the church calendar. These occasions were celebrated with colorful processions, plays, singing and dancing, music, and plentiful food and drink. The disorder that accompanied festivals was tolerated and was a useful way for people to let off steam and escape from the drudgery of their daily lives. The most wildly celebrated festival of all was Mardi Gras, which means "Fat Tuesday" in French. It took place on Shrove Tuesday before the start of Lent, the 40-day period of fasting before Easter. During Mardi Gras the world was turned on its head. Masters served servants, men dressed as women, figures of authority were mocked, and all were presided over by the Lord of Misrule, a person elected to organize the festivities. In towns festivals were often dominated by craft

guilds, the organizations that regulated crafts and professions. They organized processions and pageants, and each guild marched in its own distinctive costume. Other festivals reinforced the loyalty that people felt for the area they lived in.

Above: A late 16th-century painting showing the raucous revelry of a village festival.

Left: This late 16th-century painting shows a bustling market scene. It is packed full of peasants selling livestock, meat, eggs, fruit and vegetables, and pots and pans.

stonemasons, stood at the city's central crossroads as early as 5:00 A.M., hoping to get a day's work. The workrooms, shops, and counting houses opened their doors for business. The working day ended by 7:00 P.M., and the night curfew began an hour later.

General weekly markets, when peasants brought their produce into the city from all over the countryside, were a hubbub of activity, attracting street entertainers, actors, fortune tellers, conjurors, and medicine-selling quacks, as well as beggars. Weekly wages were paid on Saturday, when work stopped early, and the inns did a roaring trade. As in the countryside, Sunday was a day of rest. Respectable city burghers (wealthier citizens), decked out in their finest clothes, attended church. Inns and shops that opened their doors on Sundays, despite official prohibitions, attracted less-respectable citizens.

SEE ALSO

♦ Agriculture
♦ Children
♦ Food and Drink
♦ Houses
♦ Palaces and Villas
♦ Plague and Disease
♦ Population
♦ Towns

THE LIFE OF A WEALTHY MERCHANT

The thriving commerce of the Renaissance era was reflected in the growing wealth of merchants and bankers. Many enjoyed lifestyles and possessions that rivaled those of the nobility. Merchants' houses were generally located in the center of cities, fronting the main square or market. They were built from stone, brick, or timber framing to elaborate designs and had large glass windows, a very expensive luxury. Inside they had many rooms, and spaces for living and entertaining were separate. They were furnished with a vast array of possessions, including elegant furniture, vast canopied beds with feather mattresses, fine linen, wooden cabinets and chests, wall hangings, paintings, mirrors, silverware, and Oriental rugs. The diet of merchants and their families was rich in meat, game, and fish. They ate lavish meals at elegant tables laid with cloths and napkins made from damask (a type of patterned velvet) and using knives and forks—forks were only just becoming common. Like the nobility, merchants were generous patrons of the arts and also made lavish gifts to religious foundations as a way of safeguarding their souls in the afterlife.

Dante

Dante Alighieri (1265–1321) was the greatest Italian poet of the Middle Ages and is now regarded as one of the most important writers in the whole of Western literature. His poems, especially his masterpiece *The Divine Comedy*, are still read and studied today. Though he lived and died before the period we describe as the Italian Renaissance, Dante was an important role model for many writers who came after him.

Dante was born and lived most of his life in the great Italian city-state of Florence. When Dante was nine years old, his father took him to a party where he met a beautiful girl the same age as himself. Her name was Beatrice.

He wrote later that he knew that his life would be dominated by his love for her from then on.

While Dante and Beatrice both married other people, Dante retained an idealized, or courtly, love for Beatrice. This love provided the inspiration for his first great work, a collection of poems linked together by prose narratives called *La Vita Nuova* ("The New Life"). Published in 1293, the poems were written over a period of about 10 years, and they tell the story of Dante's unspoken, unacknowledged love for Beatrice. Dante was in the middle of writing one such poem when news reached him in 1290 that Beatrice had died. The poem was never finished. Dante was plunged into grief.

Left: A 15th-century painting of Dante holding a copy of his famous poem **The Divine Comedy.** *Scenes from the poem are shown behind him on the left side of the picture. The city of Florence is shown on the right.*

THE DIVINE COMEDY

Dante's greatest work, *The Divine Comedy*, is written in the form of a religious vision or journey, a style of poem that was very popular in the Middle Ages. The narrator (storyteller), assumed to be Dante, falls asleep and dreams that he meets the soul of the Roman poet Virgil. Virgil takes him on a journey into the underworld, through hell, up through purgatory, and finally hands him over to the soul of Beatrice, who leads him through paradise. In each of these three locations Dante meets and speaks with the souls of the dead, who include many well-known poets, musicians, painters, politicians, and members of the clergy. During his journey Dante learns to reject earthly pleasures and see the purpose of life as a final, joyful union with God.

Above: Dante and Virgil meet the Greek hero Ulysses, shown burning in hell.

After Beatrice's death Dante began to take an increasing interest in politics. For years Florence had been torn apart by bitter political disputes. At the time of Dante's birth the disputes had been between supporters of the pope, known as Guelfs, and supporters of the Holy Roman emperor, known as Ghibelines. The Guelfs had won, but they in turn had divided into two factions, the White Guelfs and the Black Guelfs. Dante was a White Guelf; and when the Black Guelfs seized power in 1301, he found himself in considerable danger. He was exiled the following year.

EXILE AND DISILLUSIONMENT

This was the beginning of the most unhappy period in Dante's life. He was separated from both his beloved city and his family. He was forced to wander from place to place, dependent on the goodwill of friends or the charity of great lords. He was angry and disillusioned, but he channeled his energies into his writing. The result was a second collection of poems, called the *Convivio* ("Banquet"). In contrast to the love poems of *La Vita Nuova*, the *Convivio* concentrated on moral and philosophical issues. Importantly, it was written not in Latin, but in the common language of Tuscany, which meant that more people could read it.

In 1308, despite his difficulties, Dante began his greatest masterpiece, *The Divine Comedy*. He had still not finished this great poem when Count Guido Novello da Polenta invited him to the city of Ravenna in 1317 and gave him a house to live in. Dante's wanderings were over. He finished the poem in 1321, shortly before his death. Count Guido gave him a lavish public funeral at which he gave a speech acknowledging Dante as the father and guiding light of Italian letters.

SEE ALSO

♦ Boccaccio
♦ Florence
♦ Italy
♦ Literature
♦ Petrarch
♦ Poetry

Decorative Arts

The term "decorative arts" applies to a wide range of objects designed to be both beautiful and useful. Today the word is used to distinguish items such as pieces of furniture and china from paintings and sculptures, which are called the "fine arts." In the Middle Ages, and for much of the Renaissance, such a distinction did not exist. Pieces of fine metalwork, woodwork, china, glass, and textiles were as highly valued as paintings and sculptures, and many artists were involved in producing both types of work.

Above: This magnificent gold saltcellar, which is about 12 in. (30cm) long, was made by the Italian artist Cellini in 1543. It was created for King Francis I of France and is one of the most famous pieces of decorative art produced in the Renaissance.

Pieces of decorative art were produced for the church, which had been the major patron of the arts since the Middle Ages, and increasingly for secular (nonreligious) patrons such as kings, dukes, merchants, and bankers. Decorative art made for the church included magnificent stained-glass windows, lavish textiles to hang on altars, and finely carved stone or wooden pulpits and wooden stalls (seats). Exquisite gold and silver vessels such as chalices (drinking cups used for the Communion service), reliquaries (containers for sacred relics), and monstrances (vessels for holding the consecrated host used in Communion) were among the most precious pieces of religious art.

Many of the beautiful objects used to adorn churches and to perform religious rituals were gifts from wealthy secular patrons, and in the Renaissance such people also commissioned a growing number of decorative items for their homes. The courts of ruling families, such as the Este in Ferrara and the Sforza in Milan, and the palaces of wealthy merchants and bankers that were springing up in all the major economic centers created a demand for furniture, tableware, and tapestries.

Many materials and techniques were used to make decorative objects. Valuable materials such as gold, silver,

Courts and palaces created a demand for furniture, tableware, and tapestries

and precious stones were especially prized, and goldsmiths enjoyed the highest reputation of all craftsmen and artists. In the Renaissance techniques of glassmaking were refined, especially in Venice, and Italy became the center for the production of a type of pottery known as majolica. Intricate methods of decorating objects with complex pictures and patterns made from wood and precious stones also reached a peak during the 15th and 16th centuries.

METALWORK

Certain countries or cities became specialized centers for various types of metalwork in the Renaissance. In Italy, for example, Florence had many skilled goldsmiths, and one of the most famous pieces of decorative art from the Renaissance was made by a Florentine goldsmith called Benvenuto Cellini in 1543. It is a magnificent gold saltcellar measuring about 12 in. (30cm) in length, with two elegant gold figures on top representing the sea and earth. A boat next to the bearded male figure representing the sea holds the salt, and a temple next to the female figure of earth holds the pepper. Such extravagant pieces of tableware were popular in the Renaissance, when lavish banquets were a means of impressing guests. Elaborate candlesticks, gold and silver plate, ornate textiles, glass, china, saltcellars, and food sculptures were all part of the display.

MAJOLICA

Until the late Middle Ages the most sophisticated ceramics (pottery) had come from China and the Islamic world. Spain, which was part of the Islamic Empire, was a major center and produced a type of pottery known as majolica that took its name from the Majorcan traders who exported it across Europe (Majorca is a Spanish island). Majolica was made from earthenware, a soft clay fired at a low temperature, which was covered with a

---

Extravagant tableware was a means of impressing guests

---

white glaze made from tin oxide and then decorated. Italian potters copied this pottery, and in the 15th and 16th centuries Italy became the major center of majolica production. Early majolica was decorated with only a few colors (usually green and purple on a white base) and simple patterns or pictures. However, the range of colors soon widened, and designs became more elaborate; by the 16th century they were often freely adapted from prints and paintings, with complex groups of figures and landscape backgrounds. Stories from the Bible and classical (ancient Greek and Roman) literature were among the subjects depicted.

Majolica was made in factories in various parts of Italy, including Siena, Urbino, and Venice; and many different types of product were made, including both practical tableware intended for everyday use and pieces that were designed entirely for show. Large sets of majolica were commissioned by aristocratic patrons in Italy and abroad who often specified the decoration and inclusion of their family coats of arms.

Above: A majolica plate made in 1515 in Castel Durante, Italy. It is decorated with a scene of Roman soldiers and buildings, and includes the coat of arms of Piero Ridolfi, for whom the plate was made.

Among the display pieces were large plates that were sometimes exchanged as engagement gifts and were often decorated with scenes relating to the theme of love.

During the 16th century other countries began producing pottery in imitation of majolica. In northern Europe such pottery was often called faience, a name that derives from the Italian town of Faenza, a major center of majolica production.

INTARSIA

A decorative technique called intarsia, in which small pieces of variously colored wood were used to create patterns and pictures, was also an Italian speciality in the Renaissance. Intarsia panels were used to decorate walls and furniture. The earliest examples date from the 14th century, when they were used to decorate choir stalls, the seats occupied by the singers who perform the musical parts of religious services. As the technique developed, craftsmen skillfully imitated the appearance of paintings, and many also exploited the newly discovered effects of perspective.

In terms of skill and popularity intarsia reached its peak between about 1450 and 1510. The most famous examples were commissioned by Duke Federigo II da Montefeltro in the 1470s to decorate a tiny room called a *studiolo* in his palace at Urbino in Italy. The *studiolo*, which is Italian for "little study," was an important room in Renaissance palaces and was used as a study and library. The subjects shown in the intarsia panels of Federigo's *studiolo* include arms, armor, books, writing implements, and musical and scientific instruments, which were intended to reflect all the aspects of a princely life. Details such as a bowl of

fruit and a squirrel nibbling a nut were also included. They were all skillfully represented in a trompe l'oeil effect (which is French for "tricking the eye") to create the illusion that they are piled up on the shelves of open cupboards.

PIETRE DURE

Another form of decoration at which Italian craftsmen excelled during the Renaissance was *pietre dure*, which means "hard stones" in Italian. The term is applied to intricate mosaics made from precious and semiprecious stones such as agate, chalcedony, jasper, and porphyry that were designed to decorate furniture, vases, and bowls. The stones used were very hard and had to be worked with special tools

Above: Part of the intarsia decoration (about 1472–1476) in the studiolo of the ducal palace in Urbino, Italy. This picture is actually a flat panel inlaid with different pieces of wood to look like an open cupboard stuffed full of books, candlesticks, and an hourglass.

similar to those used for cutting diamonds and other gems. They vary greatly in color, making possible a wide range of tones and effects. Italian craftsmen revived the techniques of the ancient Romans, who had been highly skilled at working in *pietre dure*, and took the technique to other parts of Europe, particularly Paris and Prague.

The best-known use of *pietre dure* is for pictorial panels that at first sight are easily mistaken for paintings due to the great skill and subtlety with which the craftsmen have cut and shaped the stones. These panels were often used as table tops and sometimes to decorate other pieces of furniture, such as cabinets. They often featured pictures of birds, flowers, and later, intricate views of Italian towns and Roman remains. Occasionally *pietre dure* was also used to embellish whole rooms, the most spectacular example being the Cappella dei Principi (Chapel of the Princes) in the church of San Lorenzo in Florence (begun 1604).

The Chapel of the Princes was a funeral chapel for the Medici family, and the *pietre dure* made for it was produced in a special workshop established by Duke Ferdinando I de Medici in 1588 called the Opificio delle Pietre Dure (Workshop of Hard Stones). This workshop still exists, and Florence continues to be the main center for this luxury craft.

Above: A view of Livorno harbor, Italy, made in **pietre dure** *in 1604. The picture was created to decorate the top of a table.*

SEE ALSO

♦ Cellini
♦ Glass
♦ Guilds and Crafts
♦ Miniatures
♦ Palaces and Villas
♦ Tapestries

Diplomacy

Diplomacy can be defined as the act of negotiation between independent states as each tries to safeguard its own interests without having to resort to war. Since ancient times rulers have used skilled negotiators to resolve any problems between them, either to bring about peace in wartime or to avoid conflict in times of peace. It was during the Renaissance period, however, that the practice, or "art," of diplomacy became a vital part of European political negotiations.

Before the Renaissance kings and princes usually sent only temporary envoys (from the French word for "someone who is sent") to other rulers. The envoys stayed only long enough to settle a treaty, arrange a royal marriage, or simply show their ruler's goodwill.

VENETIAN DIPLOMACY

The Italian city of Venice sent out many envoys to foreign rulers. Because the city depended so heavily on trade for its prosperity, Venice's rulers needed to work hard to maintain good relations with the city's trading partners. Returning envoys were also expected to give a report, called a *relazione*, about the other country's domestic affairs in case they had an effect on Venetian interests. Later, many other Italian cities and countries in Europe adopted the Venetian diplomatic system, which was much admired.

In the 14th century Italy was made up of a patchwork of independent cities, called city-states or communes.

Rivalry between the city-states meant that war was a constant threat, and the city-states' governments increasingly depended on diplomacy to keep the peace. By the end of the century a few Italian cities, such as Venice, Genoa, and Milan, were sending permanent representatives to live in the more important city-states, as well as others to the pope in Rome and the emperor of the Holy Roman Empire. At around this time such representatives came to be referred to as ambassadors.

Ambassadors were not only expected to represent their rulers and to negotiate treaties and other

Above: This 16th-century manuscript illustration shows the doge, or ruler, of Venice receiving ambassadors from the Italian city of Brescia.

THE FIELD OF THE CLOTH OF GOLD

At the beginning of June 1520 the English king Henry VIII (reigned 1507–1547) crossed the English Channel and set up a temporary palace beneath the walls of the town of Guînes, at that time an English stronghold in what is now northeastern France. Nearby, in a meadow outside the town of Ardres, Francis I (reigned 1515–1547), the king of France, set up a magnificent tent. The tent was made of gold brocade—a patterned silk—with stripes of blue velvet sprinkled with golden fleurs-de-lis, the symbol of the French monarchy.

On June 7, at the sound of a fanfare, Henry and Francis rode to meet each other at the bottom of a valley between their two camps. At first the two kings made as if to attack each other, but instead they embraced warmly. After 12 days of lavish celebrations, including feasting and tournaments, the kings attended Mass together. It was sung alternately in French and English. Henry and Francis promised to meet yearly at the same place to renew their friendship and to confirm the newly forged alliance between their countries, although they never did so. This meeting, known to historians as the Field of the Cloth of Gold, was one of the most spectacular events in the history of Renaissance diplomacy.

Above: This engraving shows Henry VIII of England (right) and Francis I of France meeting at the Field of the Cloth of Gold. The event is famous for the two rulers' extravagant displays of wealth.

agreements. They also had to keep a close watch on the affairs of their hosts—including the character of the ruler, the state of the economy, and the doings of the military—and to do so, they often used a network of spies. The role of the ambassador was, according to one Venetian diplomat, "exactly the same as any other servant of government; that is, to do, say, and think whatever may best serve the preservation and greater glory of his own state."

INTERNATIONAL EMBASSIES

By the 1460s permanent embassies were common throughout Italy. By the beginning of the following century they had also been adopted by the rulers of France, Italy, and England. In England, for example, Cardinal Thomas Wolsey (about 1475–1530) set up a diplomatic service in the 1520s. It was Cardinal Wolsey who conducted the negotiations that led to the most famous diplomatic event of the Renaissance, the meeting between Francis I of France and Henry VIII of England at the Field of the Cloth of Gold in 1520. By the 16th century rulers throughout Europe were in more or less continual communication with one another. This development also had a great cultural impact as artistic ideas spread from one country's court to another's.

The court of the pope in Rome, called the Holy See, was one of the most important centers of diplomacy during the Renaissance. The pope was not only the most powerful religious leader in Europe; he was also an influential political leader, with his own extensive territory in central Italy. There were so many ambassadors in Rome that the pope often addressed them all assembled together. Rome became a hotbed of intrigue and conspiracy, as diplomats struggled to gain the pope's support.

Above: This 15th-century painting by the artist Giacomo Pacchiarotto shows a delegation of diplomats arriving at the Italian city of Siena. The rulers of Italian cities of the Renaissance used diplomacy to seal alliances with one another.

MACHIAVELLI ON DIPLOMACY

Above: The Italian writer and diplomat Niccolò Machiavelli, who wrote extensively about the art of negotiation.

One of the most famous diplomats of the Renaissance was the Florentine Niccolò Machiavelli (1469–1527). During the early 16th century the rulers of the republic of Florence sent Machiavelli on important diplomatic missions to France, the Holy See, and the Holy Roman Empire. His skills as a hard-headed negotiator and his intelligence and courage made him an invaluable asset to the Florentine state.

In his writings on politics, including *The Prince* (1513), Machiavelli stressed the importance of diplomacy in the pursuit of a state's interests. A good ambassador, he wrote, should be able to present his case in the best possible light, omitting facts where necessary and using rhetoric (the art of speaking) to persuade his listeners. Machiavelli's writings helped gain Italy's ambassadors a reputation for underhanded, or "Machiavellian," dealings and for using language deviously. In reality, however, Italian diplomats were no less or no more straightforward than other European diplomats.

Ambassadors and other diplomatic officers were almost always aristocrats or other well-born citizens. They were always men and were usually also very highly educated. One reason why this was important was that the language used in diplomacy was Latin. Gradually, however, Latin came to be used only in formal greetings, and negotiations were conducted in ordinary languages, sometimes with the use of translators.

HAZARDS OF DIPLOMACY

Diplomacy was always hazardous in Renaissance times. As the power of states fluctuated, the political interests of rulers changed. An alliance made one year might no longer be suitable the following year. There was also a great deal of mistrust between rulers, and things could easily go wrong. For example, barely two years after his meeting with Francis I at the Field of the Cloth of Gold, Henry VIII declared war on France and launched an invasion against his former ally.

Nevertheless, the diplomatic processes laid down during the Renaissance were to prove enormously influential in the following centuries. As peace in Europe came increasingly to depend on a precarious balance of power between a few powerful states, diplomacy became an ever more essential tool in foreign policy.

Donatello

Donatello (about 1386–1466) was one of the most important Italian sculptors of the 15th century. He worked in an assured and often dramatic style that was based on a study of nature and classical (ancient Greek and Roman) art. Throughout his life he excelled at many kinds of sculpture, pioneering new techniques and reviving classical forms.

Donatello, which is short for Donato di Niccolo di Betto Bardi, was born in Florence to poor parents. When he was 17 years old, he was apprenticed to the renowned sculptor Lorenzo Ghiberti, in whose workshop he learned the techniques of modeling and bronze casting. He was also among the large team of assistants and apprentices who helped Ghiberti make the great bronze doors of the Baptistery in Florence.

BREAK WITH TRADITION

In 1408–1409, when he was about 22 years old, Donatello received his first commission, a series of marble statues to adorn the façade (front) of Florence Cathedral. These early works show Donatello thinking about sculpture in a new way as he began to break away from the elegant conventions of the popular Gothic style in search of a more lifelike approach.

In about 1415 Donatello produced his famous marble statue *Saint George* to adorn the outside of the church of Or San Michele in Florence. Unlike earlier Gothic sculptures, Donatello's statue shows that he studied the human body and was familiar with classical

Above: Donatello's sculpture Saint George *(1415) with his relief carving of Saint George fighting the dragon on the stone panel beneath.*

art. The figure is solid, the powerful hands and furrowed brow are lifelike, and the curled hair and regular facial features show the influence of Roman portrait busts (carvings).

On the frame beneath the base of the statue Donatello carved a panel of Saint George fighting the dragon. He used a new technique called *rilievo schiacciato* ("shallow relief"), in which the carving stands out less than 1 in. (2.5cm) from the background—relief carvings usually stood out much farther. The way the building and trees on the right recede into the distance also shows that Donatello was aware of developments in perspective, a mathematical system enabling artists to create a sense of space in their work.

From this time onward Donatello was much in demand, and he worked on statues, monuments, and reliefs in marble and bronze, both in Florence and farther afield in other Italian cities. Between 1430 and 1432 he visited Rome with Brunelleschi, and together they studied the city's great works of classical art.

CLASSICAL INFLUENCE

Influenced by classical sculpture, Donatello's work became even more lifelike, and it also became full of emotion. Another of his great works, an elegant bronze statue of David trampling the head of the giant Goliath, may date from this time. It was probably the first life-size male nude statue made since classical times and is one of the best-known pieces of sculpture from the Renaissance.

Donatello revived another type of classical sculpture in the 1440s when he went to work in the city of Padua. There he was asked to produce a bronze equestrian statue of Gattamelata, a famous condottiere, or mercenary soldier. Equestrian statues portray their subject sitting on horseback and in Roman times were used to commemorate emperors.

Gattamelata (about 1447–1453) was the first bronze equestrian monument of the Renaissance and was immensely influential. Donatello portrayed Gattamelata in Roman armor with a noble, idealized face and his right hand raised in a gesture of command. The sculpture itself is a great technical feat. Its huge weight is supported by three of the powerful warhorse's legs, the fourth leg is raised—as if the horse is walking forward—with the tip of its hoof resting on a sphere.

LATE WORKS

At the peak of his powers Donatello continued to pioneer new advances in sculpture. His late works, such as the wooden statues of Saint John the Baptist and Mary Magdalen, seemed rough and unfinished to people of the time, but these gaunt figures are full of emotional intensity. Donatello's work influenced many Renaissance artists, including Michelangelo and Andrea Mantegna, and today he is considered a founder of modern sculpture.

SEE ALSO

♦ Antiquities
♦ Brunelleschi
♦ Classicism
♦ Ghiberti
♦ Human Form in Art
♦ Masaccio
♦ Naturalism
♦ Perspective
♦ Sculpture

Below: Donatello's statue Gattamelata, *made between about 1447 and 1453. Donatello based his statue on an ancient Roman sculpture of the emperor Marcus Aurelius that survived in Rome.*

Drama and Theater

Left: This 17th-century painting shows a crowd watching a group of actors performing on an open-air stage. Market-places and village squares were popular locations for drama.

Renaissance Europe saw a great flowering of drama. In the Middle Ages theatrical performances had been dominated by religious themes. However, in the Renaissance drama was freed from this constraint and became a popular and accessible reflection of society as a whole.

Several countries, especially Spain and England, developed their own unique styles of theater. Specially built theaters appeared in London, Madrid, and Paris, and prolific playwrights, such as Spain's Lope de Vega (1562–1635) and England's William Shakespeare (1564–1616) and Ben Jonson (about 1573–1637), worked to satisfy the public's insatiable appetite for drama.

The Renaissance, with its emphasis on humanist teaching, originated in Italy, a country that was to make several significant contributions to theatrical development. A growing interest in the theater of ancient Rome—in particular, the plays of Terence, Plautus, and Seneca—led to the appearance of a number of plays based on these classical models.

At the same time, some of the principles of Roman theatrical design were adopted in Italy. Horseshoe-shaped theaters developed, with the stage situated at the front. Previously, a variety of different designs had been used. Italian architects also began to use painted scenery and backdrops, devices that made full use of a recent artistic discovery—perspective. The earliest, and best, example of an Italian Renaissance theater building is the Teatro Olimpico in Vicenza.

THE COMMEDIA DELL'ARTE

Classically inspired plays appealed only to a limited audience of nobles and academics. On the other hand, the Italian commedia dell'arte, or "theater of professionals," enjoyed widespread popular appeal. Its lively, improvised plays were performed by the first troupes of professional actors. They made use of stock situations and characters—the miserly merchant, the wily servant, the star-struck lover—and each actor specialized in playing a particular character. Leather half-masks were worn to denote the character portrayed.

The actors, who improvised dialogue and action around a basic plot, were highly skilled. They were required to be clowns, mimics, comedians, dancers, singers, and acrobats. The fame of the commedia dell'arte spread throughout Europe. Troupes toured in Spain, Germany, France, and England, and the influence of this early Italian theater spread to all the main national traditions.

During the Middle Ages theatrical performances in England, as in the rest of Europe, were restricted to religious drama. Mystery plays originated as part of the rituals of great Christian feasts such as Easter, perhaps as a means of educating an illiterate population. They soon moved outside the control of the church and were put on by trade guilds. The plays became more elaborate, plundering the Bible for stories such as those of Jonah and the whale and Noah's ark. Each guild was associated with a different biblical story. Importantly, they were now performed in English rather than Latin, and bawdy comic scenes intermingled with the religious drama.

Left: This 16th-century French painting shows a group of commedia dell'arte actors. This style of theater originated in Italy but became popular throughout Europe.

Frequently, mystery plays were performed in the street, from the back of a cart, or in an inn yard. Performances became increasingly elaborate and complex, with a range of props, lavish costumes, and machinery to create special effects such as clouds of smoke or floods. Mystery plays became a great popular spectacle.

In the Middle Ages troupes of players, or actors, had moved from town to town, living a hand-to-mouth existence. However, by the 16th century nobles and rich men were beginning to maintain their own troupes as parts of their household. The actors were often required to perform masques. Masques were elaborate court spectacles that mixed drama, dance, and music. They generally took their themes from classical myths and legends, and were lavishly staged.

ENGLISH THEATER

In 1576 James Burbage, a part-time actor and carpenter, built London's first permanent public theater at Finsbury Fields, simply called "the theater." The great age of Elizabethan theater had begun. Over the next few years a number of theaters appeared in London. The most famous were the Curtain, Rose, Swan, Globe, Fortune, and Hope. Groups of professional actors, under the patronage of noblemen, entertained a demanding and discriminating public. There were no women actors, however. Young boys played the female leads, while older men took on comic female roles.

A number of great playwrights emerged in the late 16th century. Christopher Marlowe (1564–1593) was a Cambridge-educated poet who abandoned the short rhyming verses of medieval drama and paved the way for Shakespeare's use of blank, or un-

rhymed, verse. His finest play was *The Tragedy of Doctor Faustus*. Another great playwright of the Elizabethan era was Ben Jonson, who had a thorough knowledge of classical authors. Among his most popular plays were his comedies *Bartholomew Fair* and *Volpone*. The greatest playwright of all, however, was William Shakespeare.

Born in 1564 in Stratford-upon-Avon, Shakespeare went to London as a young man and became an actor for a company known as the Lord Chamberlain's Men. He went on to write 37 plays that varied greatly in

Above: This sketch is of a costume designed by Bernardo Buontalenti for the masque La Pellegrina. *Masques were spectacular dramas performed at court. They were famous for their extravagant costumes and scenery.*

THE GLOBE THEATER

The Globe Theater was built in London on the south bank of the Thames River between 1598 and 1599. It was a circular playhouse, the center of which was unroofed. A raised platform stage, open on three sides, projected into an open space for standing spectators, known as "groundlings." This space was surrounded by two or three galleries, covered by a thatched roof and equipped with benches and stools. Behind the stage there was a wall in which two or three doors opened from backstage. The wall supported a gallery for musicians or actors and a tower housing machinery. The stage was covered by a canopy, and during performances a flag flew from the top of the tower. Seat prices ranged from a penny (for the groundlings) to sixpence.

The Globe was the home of the Lord Chamberlain's Men, and Shakespeare himself must have acted there many times. Among his own plays performed at the Globe were *King Lear*, *Othello*, and *Romeo and Juliet*. In 1611 the thatched roof was accidentally set alight by a cannon, and the entire theater was destroyed, although it was rebuilt just a year later. A reconstructed Globe was built in London in the 1990s.

Above: A present-day performance of Shakespeare's The Tempest *at the reconstructed Globe Theater in London.*

style and scope. Their themes range from comedy to tragedy to romance to history. The history plays tell stories from the past and address issues such as the divine right of kings and the nature of power, while the tragedies, such as *Hamlet* and *King Lear*, tackle universal themes like love, hate, jealousy, ambition, guilt, and betrayal.

THE SPANISH THEATER

In 16th-century Spain professional theatrical touring companies began to travel to noblemen's houses or from town to town. In towns they acted in inn yards or in the courtyards between buildings, known as *corrales*. Specially built theaters began to appear in the second half of the 16th century. As in London, audiences stood in an open courtyard or sat in tiered galleries. However, the most important Spanish theaters were in Madrid—the Corral de la Cruz, built in 1579, and the Corral del Principe, built in 1582. Like many English theater companies, Spanish actors were kept on yearly contracts and paid a salary by the owner of the theater.

Spanish actors were clearly influenced by their Italian counterparts in the commedia dell'arte. However, in the late 16th century a distinctive Spanish type of theater began to emerge, distinguished by its passionate and romantic style.

Spain's most famous playwright was Lope de Vega. He is credited with writing an astounding 1,800 plays, although only 430 survive. He dealt with a wide range of subject matter. Some of his plays had religious themes, while others were social comedies. Many of his comedies revolved around the contrast between the wicked town and the virtuous countryside. Vega also wrote many "cloak-and-dagger" plays, which centered on political intrigue.

SEE ALSO

♦ Literature
♦ Poetry
♦ Shakespeare

Drawing

Artists have always produced drawings, although only a small number have survived from before the middle of the 15th century. It was at this time that paper, on which most drawings are now made, became widely available in Europe. Artists used a variety of materials, including pen and ink and chalk, to produce quick sketches, careful studies from nature, and drawings that were finished pieces of art in their own right. Dürer, Leonardo da Vinci, Raphael, and Michelangelo took the practice of drawing to new heights and produced some of the greatest drawings ever made.

Before paper was manufactured on a wide scale in Europe in the 15th century, artists used parchment to draw on. Parchment was made from the skins of animals, usually sheep or calves. It is strong and durable, but also expensive to make. Therefore artists used it sparingly, mainly for drawings of standard figures or patterns that could be kept in their workshops for reference. Although paper was also costly, it was much cheaper than parchment and was therefore used more freely by artists.

Above: A drawing of praying hands made by the German artist Dürer in 1508.

CARTOONS

Today the word "cartoon" is usually applied to humorous drawings, but originally it referred to something quite different: a full-scale preparatory design for a painting or other work of art. Cartoons in this sense were first used by stained-glass artists, and painters seem to have taken up the idea in the later 14th century. There were two ways of transferring the outlines of the design from the drawing to the panel or wall that was to be painted. In the first the back of the cartoon was covered in chalk, and a pointed metal instrument, or stylus, was pressed along the outlines, transferring a chalk line to the surface against which it was held. In the second method hundreds of pinpricks were made along the outlines, and a fine powder consisting of charcoal or a similar material was dusted through the holes to the surface behind.

In the middle of the 15th century most drawings were made in pen and ink or metal point, a pointed metal rod used before pencils were invented. Charcoal, made from charred sticks, was also used to draw designs for paintings onto walls or panels.

PEN AND INK

For pen-and-ink drawings artists used quill pens that were cut with a knife (a "penknife") from the feathers of geese, swans, turkeys, and crows. Sometimes artists added washes of diluted ink or watercolor paint to their designs. Many pen-and-ink drawings survive from the Renaissance, such as Botticelli's elegant illustrations to Dante's epic poem *The Divine Comedy* and Leonardo da Vinci's vigorous sketches of the natural world and his inventions. Dürer's drawing of praying hands (shown on page 35) has become one of the most famous pen-and-ink drawings from the period. In it Dürer experimented with different materials, adding white paint and using a pale blue paper for the background.

METAL POINT

Metal-point drawings were made with a pointed metal rod on paper or parchment that had been specially coated so that the metal left a trace on it. The most commonly used metals were silver and lead. The technique produced exquisitely delicate effects but was virtually impossible to erase and so demanded great sureness of hand. It was particularly suited to the detailed style of northern European artists such as Rogier van der Weyden and Dürer, although Italian artists also excelled in its use, particularly Leonardo da Vinci.

Along with Dürer, Leonardo da Vinci was one of the greatest draftsmen of the Renaissance. As well as working in pen and ink, metal point, and charcoal, he was also the first artist to popularize the use of chalk. Chalk encouraged a much freer style of drawing than pen and metal point, and lines and tones could be easily blended.

Above: Drawings of the male body by Michelangelo. Made in red chalk, they are studies for one of his paintings.

Chalk came in black, red (actually a browny-red color), and white, and by the end of the 16th century was one of the most popular drawing materials. It was perfect for Michelangelo's dynamic style, as can been seen from his powerful drawing of a nude (on opposite page) that was made as a study for one of the figures in the Sistine Chapel.

THE IMPORTANCE OF DRAWING

The ability to draw was crucial to being a painter or sculptor, and much of the artist's training focused on developing the skill. Apprentices often practiced on cheap clay tablets using a pointed instrument called a stylus so as not to waste expensive paper or parchment. They had to learn to copy famous classical (ancient Roman and Greek) sculptures and to work from nature.

Since the portrayal of the human body lay at the center of Renaissance art, one of the most important types of drawing artists had to master was life drawing, or drawing the nude model. Life drawing was an important part of the artist's training, and painters and sculptors continued to work direct from the life model throughout their careers. Some, like Leonardo da Vinci, took their search to understand the structure of the human body further, producing careful anatomical studies of the muscles, bones, and tendons that lie below the skin.

Artists also produced preparatory drawings to work out their ideas for pictures, sculptures, and the decorative objects that they were called on to design. Most drawings that survive from the Renaissance are of this type. Because pictures usually consisted of many different elements (including figures, costumes, landscapes, and buildings), painters made both detailed studies and more general sketches to work out how to arrange the different parts. They also produced preparatory drawings for tapestries, furniture, and other decorative items that were then made either in their workshop or by other specialized craftsmen.

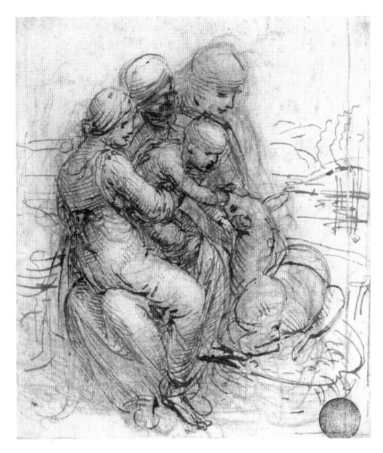

Less commonly artists made highly finished presentation drawings. Some were intended to show a patron what a finished picture or sculpture would look like, and others were intended as complete artworks in themselves. Michelangelo made several drawings of this type and presented them to friends and patrons as gifts.

By the middle of the 16th century drawings had become highly prized by collectors. The first great collection was assembled by the painter and art historian Giorgio Vasari, who valued drawings both for their artistic value and because they showed the workings of the artist's mind.

Above: Leonardo da Vinci made this drawing in about 1501–1507 to work out how to arrange the figures in one of his paintings.

SEE ALSO

♦ Anatomy
♦ Artists' Workshops
♦ Botticelli
♦ Dürer
♦ Human Form in Art
♦ Leonardo da Vinci
♦ Michelangelo
♦ Raphael
♦ Vasari

Dress

In the Renaissance the richest and most important people wore very extravagant clothes, made from velvets, silks, and rare furs, and decorated with gold and gems. Dress was such an important way in which people displayed their status that in many places rules called sumptuary laws were passed to control what different sorts of people—such as various ranks of the nobility and merchants—could wear.

The Renaissance saw a vast array of fashions and luxurious clothes for the wealthy. At the beginning of the period young men began to discard the long overcoat worn in the Middle Ages in favor of a padded, quilted jacket called a doublet or pourpoint. It was worn with woolen hose (stockings), although silk stockings became popular in the 16th century. At this time hose were also divided into upper and lower hose. Upper hose were effectively shorts and were often padded and slashed to reveal insets of brightly colored silk. Lower hose covered the lower leg.

Shoes were leather, pointed, and buttoned or laced. In the 15th century there was a fashion for shoes called poulaines, which had exaggeratedly long points. The points grew so long that eventually they often stuck up as high as 2 ft (60cm) and had to be supported by whalebone. Men also wore fur-trimmed cloaks and a variety of hats made of felt or beaver skin. An expanding array of textiles and fabric dyes reflected Renaissance Europe's growing links with the rest of the

world. Silks, satins, and velvets were colored with scarlet and cochineal from Armenia, indigo from Baghdad or Bengal, and saffron from India.

During the Renaissance fashions for women became increasingly rigid and exaggerated. At the beginning of the period gowns were fitted around the upper body, but were otherwise loose and flowing, with wide sleeves and low necklines. Gradually, women began to wear tight, laced bodices lined with

Left: This portrait of King Charles IX of France was painted in about 1565. It shows him in lavish clothes that reflect his status. He wears a doublet and cloak of black velvet embroidered with gold, a shirt and hose made from silk, and a lace ruff.

SUMPTUARY LAWS

Sumptuary laws regulated what people could wear. In some cases they reflected the disapproval of the church for fashions such as low-cut necklines for women. In others they were designed to keep people such as merchants in their place by denying them luxury fabrics considered appropriate only for people of noble birth. On some occasions the laws were simply put in place to stem the demand for rare materials, mainly fur.

Right: This portrait of Catherine de Medici, regent of France, shows her in the fashionable dress of the 16th century. Her waist is nipped in, and her sumptuous, full-skirted dress is split at the front to reveal yet more rich fabric beneath.

canvas and edged with wire. They wore stiff, bell-shaped underskirts called farthingales, to make their skirts look full, and increasingly elaborate pleated and lace-trimmed collars, called ruffs, which were also worn by men.

The influence of the Spanish court, which spread all over Europe in the 16th century, introduced a fashion for dark, somber colors. The Holy Roman emperor Charles V and his son King Philip II of Spain always dressed in black, and it became a popular color for both men and women's clothes—in marked contrast to the exuberant, bright colors of the 15th century.

DISPLAYS OF WEALTH

Clothes were one way people could show off their wealth and status. In 1363, for example, Simon Peruzzi, a wealthy Italian banker, gave his wife a tunic lined with squirrel skin and decorated with silver buttons and gold stripes. It cost the equivalent of 140 days' wages for a stonemason. An elaborate wedding dress belonging to another Italian banking family, the Strozzi, cost the equivalent of 550 days' wages for a skilled laborer. The dress was decorated with 200 peacock-tail feathers, pearls, and gilt leaves.

The elderly, members of the church and the legal profession, and academics

SEE ALSO
♦ Courts and Court Culture
♦ Textiles

dressed in a more restrained way. They retained the knee-length overcoats of the Middle Ages, usually in dark colors, such as black, crimson, and violet.

Peasants wore brown or gray tunics or dresses over hose. In winter they wore fur-lined, hooded cloaks to keep them warm. The best fur a peasant could hope for was rabbit or cat. In general, men's hoods were blue and women's red. Underclothing consisted of a chemise, which was a loose shirt, for women and long underpants for men, all made from coarse woolen cloth. Wooden clogs protected their feet from mud and dirt. Clothes were made to last, and many people had only two sets that they washed only occasionally. As a result their clothes were usually ill-fitting, dirty, and worn.

Dürer

Albrecht Dürer (1471–1528) was the leading artist in Germany at the beginning of the 16th century and did more than any other artist to bring the ideas of the Italian Renaissance to northern Europe. He was best known as a printmaker, but his oil paintings were also highly sought after, and he created some of the most beautiful drawings and watercolors of the Renaissance.

Dürer was born in May 1471 in the German town of Nuremberg, where his father was a goldsmith. Initially Dürer worked in his father's workshop, but he showed such skill at drawing that he was apprenticed to Michael Wolgemut, a German artist who made woodcuts to

Dürer sought to raise the regard in which he and other artists were held

illustrate books. When he completed his apprenticeship, Dürer spent four years traveling, during which time he worked for printmakers in Switzerland and Germany. In 1494 he returned to Nuremberg and married Alice Frey.

Soon afterward Dürer set out on the first of two trips to Italy to study artistic developments there. He visited Pavia and Venice, and was stimulated by the creative environment he found. He learned about perspective and was influenced by the way that Italian

painters portrayed the human body both by studying nature and by applying theories about ideal beauty and proportions based on classical (ancient Greek and Roman) art. His interest in portraying the human body is most clearly seen in his engraving *Adam and Eve* (1504).

A GREAT PRINTMAKER

When he returned to Nuremberg in 1495, Dürer set up a workshop and concentrated on establishing his reputation. Many of his finest works were prints, and he did much to develop the medium. Prints were made by either carving a design into a wooden block (woodcuts) or cutting a line into a metal plate (engravings and

Above: Dürer painted this Self-Portrait *in 1500. He shows himself with a serene but solemn face framed by long ringlets of hair. Painters often depicted Christ in a similar way. By portraying himself like this, Dürer emphasized his "god-given" gifts as an artist.*

etchings). Compared to paintings, they were cheap to make and could be produced in large numbers.

The Apocalypse (1498) is the most celebrated of Dürer's early prints and consists of a set of woodcuts that illustrates the Book of Revelation from the Bible. Among his most famous engravings are *The Knight, Death, and the Devil* (1513), which is about the power of the Christian faith; *Saint Jerome in His Study* (1514); and *Melancolia I* (1514), a portrayal of the relationship between melancholy and creativity. All of Dürer's prints have highly inventive imagery and are both powerful and detailed. He continually experimented with different print-making techniques, but his prints were always skillfully executed.

SEE ALSO
◆ Drawing
◆ German Art
◆ Human Form in Art
◆ Prints

Below: Dürer's engraving **The Knight, Death, and the Devil** *(1513). It shows a knight being taunted by a horrible skeletal figure of death (who holds an hourglass) and a dragonlike devil.*

The detail evident in Dürer's prints typified the rest of his art. He thought that it was important for artists to study nature and produced many beautiful, carefully observed studies of landscapes, flowers, birds, animals, and the human body. Some of his best-known works are watercolor studies of a hare (1502) and a piece of turf (1503), and a drawing of a pair of praying hands (1508—see page 35).

RAISING THE STATUS OF ARTISTS

On his second trip to Italy from 1505 to 1507 Dürer was struck by the high status enjoyed by Italian painters compared to German artists, who were looked down on as craftsmen. He sought to raise the regard in which he and other artists were held. He studied classical literature, mathematics, and geometry, and toward the end of his life wrote books on a wide range of subjects, including perspective and proportion. He also emphasized his status in two of the many self-portraits he made. In one he portrayed himself as a nobleman in front of an open window (1498) and in another in a Christlike pose (1500), intended to emphasize his own "godlike" gifts.

Although Dürer felt that artists were underappreciated in Germany, he was much in demand. In 1509 he was able to purchase an impressive house in Nuremberg, and in 1512 he was appointed court painter to the Holy Roman emperor Maximilian I. When Maximilian died, Dürer traveled to Aachen in 1520 to meet his successor, Charles V, and win his patronage. He journeyed on to the Netherlands and Belgium, where he was honored by artists wherever he went. By the time of his death in 1528 he was esteemed by artists and patrons in both northern Europe and Italy.

Eastern Europe

During the Renaissance eastern Europe was important as a region that produced surplus cereals and vital raw materials. The forests of what are now Poland and north-eastern Germany provided large amounts of timber, as well as animal skins for furs and leather, beeswax for candles, and honey, which was used as a sweetener. There were also vast plains in the area, where large amounts of grain grew. To the south were the Carpathian Mountains of Hungary, which contained rich veins of many kinds of metallic ores as well as deposits of salt.

Goods from eastern Europe were transported to the west, where extra food was required to maintain increasingly specialized workers, who in turn transformed the raw materials from the east into finished products. Since land and resources were plentiful in eastern Europe, but labor was in short supply, nobles and other

Left: The Barbakan castle in Krakow, built in 1498. Located on the Vistula River, Krakow was the capital of Poland, one of the most powerful states in eastern Europe during the period of the Renaissance.

landowners kept their labor force from moving by tying them to the land. This relationship, in which a peasant farmer and his descendants worked a certain piece of land and were not allowed to leave without their lord's permission, was known as serfdom. Serfdom increased in eastern Europe during the Renaissance period, even though it was declining in the west at the same time.

The eastern Europe of the Renaissance was inhabited by people from a variety of different groups and cultures, who spoke a number of different languages and practiced a wide range of religions. Among the groups who lived in the region were Slavs, Germans, Hungarians, and Albanians, all of whom spoke different languages. The area was home to both Roman Catholic and Orthodox Christians, as well as Yiddish-speaking Jews who had begun moving east from Germany to settle in Bohemia and Poland. In the 14th, 15th, and 16th centuries the invading Turkish Muslims from the Ottoman Empire added to the religious mix. When the Protestant Reformation occurred in western Europe in the 16th century, an additional flood of ideas and immigrants swept eastward.

POLAND AND LITHUANIA

In the middle of the 14th century the political situation in eastern Europe changed as new states rose to power. The first development was the growth of a strong kingdom in Poland, which had practically disappeared during the 13th century. The man behind this recovery was King Casimir III (ruled 1333–1370), otherwise known as Casimir the Great. He reorganized both the country's army and its government and was wise enough to pursue a policy of avoiding conflict with his most

powerful neighbors, the Teutonic Knights to the north and the kingdom of Bohemia to the southwest. Meanwhile, he expanded the region under his control to the southeast along the slopes of the Carpathian Mountains of northern Hungary.

In 1385 one of the most important events in the history of Poland occurred when the country formed an alliance with the grand duchy of Lithuania. By the end of the 14th century the region of Poland-Lithuania stretched from the Baltic to the Black Sea. The first ruler of this area was Vladislav II (1351–1434), the grand duke of Lithuania, who acquired the Polish crown by agreeing to convert his still pagan Lithuanian subjects to Roman Christianity.

The union of Poland and Lithuania was largely brought about by events in the neighboring country of Hungary.

Above: This map shows the major states in eastern Europe in the mid-15th century, as well as some of the most important cities and battles (marked with crossed swords).

In 1308 the Hungarian nobles elected a foreigner from the French Angevin family to become King Charles I (1288–1342). By encouraging foreign miners to settle in the Carpathian Mountains, Charles helped develop Hungary's mining industry. However, Charles also lost much Hungarian territory to Venice and Serbia.

LOUIS THE GREAT

Charles' son Louis the Great (1326–1382) was more successful in war. The nephew of the Polish king Casimir the Great, Louis regained control over the kingdom of Croatia and, most importantly, the rich cities of Dalmatia. Following the death of the Serbian ruler Stephen Dusan (1308–1355), he reasserted Hungarian influence in the Balkans and brought the region of Moldavia under his control. The height of Louis's power was reached in 1370, when he succeeded his uncle as king of Poland. The Polish aristocracy, however, refused to accept Louis's own successor, Sigismund (1368–1437), leading them to turn to Vladislav of Lithuania instead.

The reign of Sigismund saw a decline in Hungarian fortunes. The Ottoman Turks expanded relentlessly in the Balkans. In 1456, however, the great Hungarian military leader János Hunyadi (about 1397–1456) managed to stop Turkish armies at Belgrade. This victory won him fame throughout Europe and halted the Ottoman advance for 50 years. Hunyadi's son Matthias Corvinus (1443–1490) later became king of Hungary.

During the first half of the 14th century Serbia seemed destined to replace the declining Byzantine Empire

Below: This painting shows Louis the Great of Hungary leading his forces to victory against a Bulgarian army. As well as being king of Hungary, Louis also inherited the Polish throne from his uncle Casimir the Great.

HUNGARY'S RENAISSANCE PRINCE

From 1458 to 1490 King Matthias Corvinus ruled Hungary in the style of an Italian Renaissance prince. An educated ruler, he did much to promote humanist learning. The humanists were scholars who looked back to the art and writings of ancient Greece and Rome for their inspiration. Matthias brought in many humanists from abroad and also encouraged scholars from Hungary itself, such as Janus Pannonius. In his capital city of Buda Matthias established a Renaissance palace with a magnificent library. He placed it under the charge of the German mathematician Regiomontanus, whose techniques of stellar navigation were used by Christopher Columbus.

Matthias himself had no royal blood—his father was the famous general János Hunyadi, who had led the Hungarians to many victories over the Turks—so he was eager to use humanist scholarship to justify his reign. He employed the Italian Antonio Bonfini to write a long history of the Hungarians, beginning from their settlement in the Carpathian Basin in around 900 A.D. Although some of this work is based on authentic documents, other parts are pure fiction, most notably the section that seeks to trace the Hunyadi family tree back to the Romans.

Left: A marble relief of Matthias Corvinus, the work of an unknown Italian sculptor.

as the leading state in the Eastern Orthodox world. Serbia reached its height during the reign of Stephen Dusan, who conquered most of the Balkan peninsula and in 1346 proclaimed himself emperor of the Serbs, Greeks, Bulgarians, and Albanians. The Ottomans, however, quickly reversed Serbian gains following Stephen's death, forcing them out of Thrace in 1371 and then defeating the Serbs decisively on their own ground at the famous battle of Kosovo in 1389.

OTTOMAN CONQUEST

The victory at Kosovo opened the way for the Turkish conquest of the entire Balkan peninsula, a prospect that caused much fear among the rulers of western Europe. In 1396 a crusade was launched against the Turks under the leadership of Sigismund. However, it ended in disaster at the battle of Nicopolis the same year. For a while the Ottomans ruled Serbia indirectly through cooperative local officials. However, after 1459 Hungarian pressure forced the sultan to govern Serbia directly, with the exception of Belgrade, which had been recaptured by Hungary three years earlier.

The Ottomans made few new conquests in eastern Europe in the second half of the 15th century. After 1500, however, a new wave of Ottoman expansion began. The most spectacular gains came during the reign of Suleyman the Magnificent (ruled 1520–1566), when the sultan's armies decisively crushed the Hungarians at the battle of Mohács in 1526. This event led to the Turkish conquest of most of the traditional

Hungarian kingdom. Because King Louis II was killed in the battle, it also led to a change in the royal dynasty.

Louis was succeeded by Ferdinand of Austria (1503–1564), the brother of the Holy Roman emperor Charles V. Although Ferdinand only controlled a narrow strip of Hungarian territory, he successfully defended his lands and eventually established his dynasty's claim to rule Hungary, Croatia, and Bohemia, laying the foundation for the Hapsburg Empire in eastern Europe.

North of the Carpathian Mountains Poland seemed to be reemerging as a major power at approximately the same time as Hungarian fortunes were in decline. In 1525 Poland absorbed the

Left: Ottoman troops under the command of Suleyman the Magnificent set off for the conquest of Hungary. Suleyman's military campaigns brought much of Hungary under his control.

A strong Muscovite state arose to put pressure on Lithuania

state ruled by the Teutonic Knights. This action paved the way for Polish expansion along its northeastern Baltic coast. Meanwhile, to the east a strong Muscovite state arose to put pressure on Lithuania. The rise of Muscovy coincided with Ottoman advances north of the Black Sea. These external threats to Lithuania resulted in it being officially absorbed into Poland in 1569.

RELIGIOUS CHANGES

As the political map of eastern Europe was being redrawn in the 16th century, new religious ideas were being imported from the west. The conquest of many parts of southeastern Europe by the Islamic Ottoman Turks actually helped make Protestantism spread more easily. Even though Islamic and

Christian countries had been at war with each other for many centuries, Muslim rulers generally allowed Christians and Jews to worship freely, and in the 16th century a complex situation arose in which various types of Christianity existed side by side.

To the north of the Ottoman Empire various different strands of Protestantism spread across Poland. Lutheranism and Calvinism, based on the teachings of Martin Luther and John Calvin respectively, were the most popular. Calvinism was especially attractive to the nobility because it taught that a king had no right to impose a particular religion on his subjects. The religion thus decreased a king's power in relation to that of his nobles. Other smaller and more extreme forms of Protestantism, such as Antitrinitarianism and Anabaptism, also quickly established themselves in eastern Europe.

SEE ALSO
- Bohemia
- Calvin
- Germany
- Hapsburg Family
- Humanism
- Luther
- Ottoman Empire
- Protestantism
- Russia

Education

During the 16th century there was a substantial increase in the number of schools in Europe and a change in the type of education they offered. Although many people had no schooling and were unable to read or write, the sons of rich merchants and the nobility benefited from a wide-ranging education. It focused on developing pupils' understanding of themselves and the world in which they lived, rather than training them for the church or professions, the goal of most medieval education.

The importance attached to education reflected the influence of humanism, a new way of thinking about human life that characterized the Renaissance. Humanist scholars studied Latin and Greek texts and found in them a fresh way of thinking about the world that stressed the importance of developing people as rounded, cultured individuals. Humanists stressed the role of education in this process, and many prominent philosophers wrote treatises (books) on the subject.

HUMANIST SCHOOLS

In 1402 Pietro Paolo Vergerio (1370–1444/45), an Italian humanist, wrote a treatise on what education should seek to achieve. He emphasized a balanced education in which pupils' bodies are improved by exercise just as their

THE SCHOOL DAY

The typical school day began at 7:00 A.M. and ended at 4:00 P.M., with an hour off in the middle of the day for a midday meal. Pupils had only Sundays and one afternoon a week free from study. They were taught in often crowded classrooms and sat on wooden benches that were sometimes arranged in rows according to ability. A teacher delivered lessons at the front of the classroom or read selected texts. Discipline was kept by teachers and senior students, who often used beatings to control unruly students. There were also competitions and regular exams to encourage pupils to learn. The school day included games and physical activities as well as more formal lessons.

Below: A picture of Maximilian Sforza being taught by his tutor at the Milanese court, surrounded by distractions. The Sforza family ruled Milan, Italy, for much of the Renaissance, and their court was a center for the arts and learning.

minds are improved by lessons. He stressed the importance of acquiring good communication skills (reading, writing, and speaking) and of studying history and philosophy. Vergerio felt that knowledge of these subjects helped pupils understand their own times and provided examples of how to live.

Mathematics, astronomy, and natural science were also to be studied in order to understand the world and people's place in it. These subjects were known as the "liberal arts" because they were thought to "liberate" people so that they could realize their potential.

ITALIAN SCHOOLS

A type of secondary school called the gymnasium, based on humanist ideas, emerged in Italian ducal courts in the 15th century. Nobles and members of their courts began to accept that education was a mark of civilization and a means of self-advancement. Highly educated tutors were hired to teach noble children and act as advisers to their parents, and in this way the ducal courts of Italy became important centers of humanism. A book called *The Courtier* (1528) by Baldassare Castiglione discusses the importance of a humanist education for courtiers.

In Renaissance gymnasiums the pupils' education was organized into three stages: the elementary level, at which reading and pronunciation were taught, followed by the grammatical level, and finally, the highest level, which concentrated on rhetoric, or the art of public speaking. Later lessons focused on the liberal arts; medicine, law, metaphysics, and theology were also studied. Emphasis was placed on the two great classical languages, Latin and Greek, and on physical education and recreation. Prominent humanist gymnasiums were founded in many Italian cities, in particular Padua, Verona, Mantua, and Venice.

NORTHERN EUROPE

In Holland the influential humanist scholar Erasmus (about 1466–1536) wrote a number of books that introduced the concepts of a humanist education to a wider range of people. He argued that, if adequately educated, any man could learn any discipline. Like Italian humanists, he emphasized the importance of the liberal arts and the study of classical languages and texts in education. He campaigned to improve schools and the training of teachers.

Erasmus's ideas affected education in the whole of northern Europe. In England influential humanists such as Thomas More and John Colet started a new type of school called the "grammar school"—knowledge of grammar was considered the foundation of a good education—that remained a model for centuries. Colet founded Saint Paul's School in London in 1510. It soon became a leading center of humanist education and still functions today. Over 300 new grammar schools were established in England between 1500 and 1620, and many more were founded all across Europe by cathedrals, craft guilds, hospitals, and private benefactors.

Universities had been established all over Europe from the 13th century onward, and they continued to be founded in the 15th and 16th centuries,

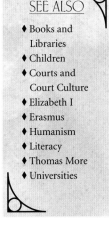

Above: A 15th-century panel from the Campanile, or bell tower, of Florence Cathedral. The panel shows two students being instructed in grammar, which was considered a fundamental part of the humanist education.

especially in northern and eastern Europe. The majority of courses still focused on professional training, such as law or medicine, as they had done in the medieval period, although the teaching of the liberal arts increased in importance. Universities were truly cosmopolitan centers, attracting many foreign students, and the connections they forged across the length and breadth of Europe encouraged the spread of humanist ideas.

THE UNEDUCATED

Despite all the advances that took place in secondary education during the Renaissance, not everyone benefited. Sons of peasants were lucky if the village priest taught them the rudiments of reading and writing— and education seemed irrelevant to children who started their working lives in the fields at the age of eight.

Girls often received no education; or if they did, it was in the skills needed to run a household. However, girls from some rich and powerful families sometimes got a broader humanist education. For example, Elizabeth I, queen of England, was renowned for her learning.

TOWNSPEOPLE AND EDUCATION

In towns levels of literacy (the ability to read and write) were higher than in the country. Craftsmen and shopkeepers needed the rudiments of reading, writing, and arithmetic to run their businesses; but beyond acquiring these basic skills, their education was professional, usually consisting of a seven-year apprenticeship in their chosen craft or trade.

Elizabeth I

Queen Elizabeth I of England (1533–1603) enjoyed a long and prosperous reign, ruling her country wisely during a period of intense international religious and political strife. During her reign music, literature, drama, and painting flourished, and the period is known as the Elizabethan era.

Elizabeth was the only daughter of Henry VIII and his second wife, Anne Boleyn, who was executed for treason when Elizabeth was just three years old. After the death of her father in 1547 Elizabeth spent the rest of her childhood in considerable danger as first her brother Edward (ruled 1547–1553) and then her half-sister Mary (ruled 1553–1558) took the throne.

Elizabeth's life was especially difficult during Mary's reign. Mary was a devout Catholic who was determined to reestablish the religion in England. She was responsible for the deaths of many Protestants, who were burned at the stake as heretics. Elizabeth found herself the focus of many plots to replace the queen; but despite the obvious threat that she posed to Mary, Elizabeth managed to survive.

After Mary died in 1558, Elizabeth became queen at the age of 25. Following the religious turmoil of the last 25 years, Elizabeth was determined to bring peace and stability to England, and her 45-year reign was characterized by shrewd political judgment. She was ably supported by loyal advisers such as Sir Francis Walsingham and Sir William Cecil.

One of Elizabeth's first steps as ruler was to pass the Acts of Supremacy and Uniformity of 1559 to reestablish the Church of England, which acknowledged the monarch rather than the pope as its head. Although many of Elizabeth's subjects remained Roman Catholics, they were not persecuted so long as they conformed outwardly and remained loyal to the queen.

THE VIRGIN QUEEN

Elizabeth's failure to marry soon became a cause of concern to Protestants. They were worried that if she died without producing an heir, the Catholics would regain control of the country—there was a strong faction of Catholics who regarded the Protestant Elizabeth as a heretic. However, Eliz-

Above: A portrait of Elizabeth painted in 1588 after England's defeat of the Spanish Armada. The queen wears a splendid gown bedecked with jewels and gold thread, and her hand rests on a globe of the world. In the background can be seen a painting of the English ships that routed the mighty Spanish Armada.

THE CULT OF GLORIANA

Elizabeth kept very careful control of the image that she presented to her subjects. When she appeared in public, Elizabeth always dressed in magnificent clothes, turning her appearances into lavish spectacles. Another way that the queen controlled her image was by limiting the number of portraits that were painted of her. Sometimes these paintings celebrated her as a mythological figure, such as the Greek goddess Diana. Poets were also eager to mythologize her. Edmund Spenser depicted her as Gloriana, Queen of the Fairies, in his epic poem *The Faerie Queen* (1596).

The cult of Gloriana, as it has since become known, greatly increased Elizabeth's political power. The image of the sumptuously dressed "Virgin Queen," married only to her country, was a very powerful one. It greatly strengthened the bond between Elizabeth and her subjects.

Above: Elizabeth on a royal progress to Westminster in about 1580. Magnificent in white and sparkling with jewels, the queen is carried on the shoulders of courtiers, surrounded by the rest of her court.

abeth was able to turn her unmarried status to her advantage, using the possibility of marriage as a diplomatic tool with which to maneuver political rivals both at home and abroad.

One person who posed a threat to Elizabeth for much of her reign was her Catholic cousin, Mary, Queen of Scots (1542–1587). Mary fled Scotland in 1568 because of political turmoil; but when she arrived in England, Elizabeth imprisoned her. Mary became the focus of several Catholic plots to overthrow Elizabeth. The last of them was the Babington Plot of 1586, which sealed Mary's fate. She was tried for treason and executed.

THE ARMADA

Meanwhile, the threat of war with Spain was ever-present. English naval captains were raiding Spanish treasure ships transporting gold from the New World, while Elizabeth was also providing financial and military support for the Dutch rebels fighting Spanish rule in the Netherlands.

In 1588 Philip II of Spain sent a great Armada (fleet) of 130 ships and 30,000 men to invade England and depose the "heretic queen." Plans to link up with an army in the Netherlands failed, and the English fleet inflicted heavy damages on the Spanish ships, which were then largely destroyed by storms on the way back to Spain. Before the encounter Elizabeth gave a rousing speech to soldiers at the port of Tilbury, declaring: "I know I have the body of a weak and feeble woman, but I have the heart and stomach of a king." It was one of the highpoints of her reign.

Elizabeth's death in 1603 marked the end of the Tudor dynasty. She was succeeded by James VI of Scotland, the Protestant son of Mary, Queen of Scots, who ruled England as James I.

SEE ALSO
♦ England
♦ Henry VIII
♦ Netherlands
♦ Philip II
♦ Protestantism
♦ Reformation
♦ Spain

England

A t the end of the 14th century England was in a state of crisis. When Richard II (ruled 1377–1399) ascended the throne at the age of 10, the country was still reeling from the aftereffects of the Black Death, which had first struck in 1348. The disease had wiped out around a third of the population. There was also considerable religious discontent. In 1375 the Oxford scholar John Wycliffe (1330–1384) had published a treatise attacking the corruption of the clergy, and his views found much popular support.

At the same time, the Hundred Years' War with France that had begun in 1337 was proving very expensive. A series of poll taxes was levied to help pay for it (a poll tax is one that is levied at a flat rate on every member of the population). The taxes met with much opposition and sparked England's first popular rebellion—the Peasants' Revolt of 1381.

The speedy spread of the Peasants' Revolt took the authorities by surprise. Armed villagers and townsmen from the south of England descended on London, which they looted and burned, killing many royal officials. The young king only persuaded the rebels to disperse after promising various reforms. He never kept his promises, although the poll tax was quietly abandoned.

In 1399 the increasingly tyrannical Richard was deposed by his cousin, Henry Bolingbroke, duke of Lancaster, following a dispute over Henry's inheritance. Henry IV (ruled 1399-1413) was faced with lengthy rebellions both in Wales and at home, which he defeated. The irregular nature of Henry's succession meant that he and his Lancastrian successors were never secure in their claim to the throne.

THE VICTORIES OF HENRY V

Nevertheless, Henry's son Henry V (ruled 1413–1422) united England's nobles in his ambition to reclaim England's lost French territories. In 1415 Henry won brilliant victories at Harfleur and Agincourt, despite being heavily outnumbered. However, his sudden death from illness placed control of England back in the hands of the nobles, who ruled on behalf of his nine-month-old son Henry VI (ruled 1422–1461 and 1470–1471).

During Henry VI's reign all of England's French conquests except Calais were lost, bringing the Hundred Years' War to an end in 1453. The blow

Above: The red rose of Lancaster, the badge adopted by the house of Lancaster in the Wars of the Roses. Henry VI is shown in the center.

to national pride, combined with the king's weak rule and a corrupt government, led to an unsuccessful popular rebellion in 1450. Five years later Henry's mental breakdown triggered a drawn-out power struggle for the crown, known as the Wars of the Roses.

THE WARS OF THE ROSES

The Wars of the Roses, so-called because the opposing sides adopted different colored roses as their badge, were fought between the house of Lancaster (a red rose), led nominally by Henry VI, and the house of York (a white rose), led by Richard, duke of York. Both sides believed that they had valid claims to the throne. First one side and then the other gained the upper hand. After years of fighting Richard's son finally claimed the throne for the house of York as Edward IV (ruled 1461–1470 and 1471–1483). Apart from one brief period when Henry VI was reinstated, the house of York held power until 1485, when Edward's brother Richard III (ruled 1483–1485) was defeated by Henry Tudor, later Henry VII (ruled 1485–1509), at the battle of Bosworth.

THE HOUSE OF TUDOR

The marriage of Henry VII to Elizabeth of York finally united both houses in a single dynasty—the Tudors. Henry was fortunate to come to the throne at a time when the English economy was booming, having long since recovered from the depression caused by plague, war, and famine that had affected the country in the 14th century. The boom was led by the textile industry. Previously the country had mainly exported raw wool. Now England also

JOHN WYCLIFFE

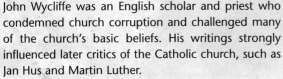

John Wycliffe was an English scholar and priest who condemned church corruption and challenged many of the church's basic beliefs. His writings strongly influenced later critics of the Catholic church, such as Jan Hus and Martin Luther.

Born in Yorkshire, Wycliffe was educated at Oxford University, where he took up a church post. Wycliffe became interested in politics and was outspsoken in the debate on whether the pope had the right to impose taxes on England. Wycliffe opposed Pope Gregory XI on this issue, causing the pope to call unsuccessfully for his arrest.

Wycliffe then began a more thorough attack on the church. His particular target was the doctrine of transubstantiation—the belief that during the rite of Communion the bread and wine used in the Mass become the body and blood of Christ. On a more general level he criticized both the excessive wealth of the church and the involvement of churchmen in politics. His criticisms foreshadowed the Protestant Reformation of the 16th century.

Above: The church reformer John Wycliffe, who also organized the first English translation of the Bible.

siderable amount of money at the time. On his death he left a secure throne, a relatively united kingdom, and a solvent government.

Henry's son and successor Henry VIII (ruled 1509–1547) displayed many of the virtues and vices associated with Renaissance rulers. He was eager to develop the arts, inviting both the writer Erasmus and the painter Hans Holbein the Younger to England, but at the same time waged many pointless wars. As time went on, Henry became increasingly violent, short-tempered, and suspicious. He executed many

---

During his reign Henry VII took pains to make the system of tax collection more efficient

---

leading noblemen and churchmen, as well as two of his six wives.

The key moment in Henry's reign came when he divorced his first wife, Catherine of Aragon, for failing to produce a son, marrying Anne Boleyn instead. The act caused a split between Henry and the pope, with Henry himself becoming head of the Church of England. Henry's act came at a time when Protestantism, the strand of Christianity represented by the teachings of Martin Luther and John Calvin, was becoming important in Europe. Henry's breakaway from the Catholic church led to the creation of the Anglican (English) church, which was independent of the pope.

Henry was succeeded in 1547 by his nine-year-old son Edward VI (ruled 1547–1553), who inherited a country with bitter religious divisions. During

Above: Henry VII of England, painted by an unknown artist. Henry devoted his reign to making the country secure and solvent—he has been called the best accountant to sit on the English throne. He also greatly improved the administration of his kingdom.

became a major exporter of finished woolen textiles.

This boom in the economy benefited Henry personally because the king collected duties on all exports. During his reign Henry took great pains to make the system of tax collection more efficient. He also reorganized the justice system and made it more difficult for nobles to raise private armies. Unlike many of his predecessors, Henry avoided expensive foreign wars. In 1492 he made a treaty with France in which he renounced all claims to the French throne for a one-time payment of £159,000, a con-

Edward's brief reign power was really held by two nobles, called lord protectors—Edward Seymour, duke of Somerset, and John Dudley, earl of Warwick. Dudley's attempts to impose Protestantism failed. When Edward was succeeded by his half-sister Mary (ruled 1553–1558), she restored the Catholic church and authorized the burning of over 300 Protestants. Her religious intolerance earned her the nickname "Bloody Mary."

ELIZABETHAN ENGLAND

By contrast, the long and prosperous reign of Mary's half-sister Elizabeth I (ruled 1558–1603) brought much-needed peace and stability to England during a period of international religious and political conflict. Elizabeth quickly restored the Protestant Church of England, but promoted a policy of religious toleration among her people, the majority of whom were still Catholic. Elizabeth was still the target of several Catholic plots, which aimed to replace her with her imprisoned cousin Mary, Queen of Scots. Mary was eventually executed in 1587.

Abroad, Elizabeth made peace with France, assisted the Protestant rebels in the Netherlands, and encouraged English sailors to raid Spanish treasure ships from the New World. In 1588 her navy prevented an invasion of England by defeating the Spanish Armada.

England under Elizabeth was a place where the arts flourished. The composers John Dowland and Thomas Tallis, poets Philip Sidney and Edmund Spenser, and playwrights Christopher Marlowe, William Shakespeare, and Ben Jonson all worked during this period.

Elizabeth's death in 1603 ended the Tudor line and united the crowns of England and Scotland for the first time in the Protestant son of Mary, Queen of Scots, who became James I of England (ruled 1603–1625).

SEE ALSO
♦ Catholic Church
♦ Drama and Theater
♦ Eastern Europe
♦ Elizabeth I
♦ Francis I
♦ Henry VIII
♦ Luther
♦ More, Thomas
♦ Protestantism
♦ Reformation
♦ Religious Dissent
♦ Shakespeare

Left: A design for a tapestry showing the defeat of the Spanish Armada by the English fleet in 1588. A plan for the Spanish ships to pick up an army in the Netherlands had failed, and after being harrassed by the English navy, they retreated to Spain, many of them being wrecked in a storm on the way.

Erasmus

Desiderius Erasmus (about 1466–1536) was one of Europe's leading scholars and writers, and a symbol of tolerance and reason during a period of bitter religious strife. His work on ancient texts of the Bible produced a more accurate version of the New Testament and paved the way for many later studies of the Scriptures.

Erasmus was born in Rotterdam in the Netherlands, the illegitimate son of a priest. As a child he studied under the humanist teacher Alexander Hegius. The humanists encouraged the study of ancient Latin and Greek texts and found in them a fresh way of looking at the world, one that emphasized the importance of education and the intellectual and artistic development of the individual. This school of thought had a great influence on Erasmus's adult work.

After his parents died, Erasmus attended another, more strictly religious school, after which he entered an Augustinian monastery, where he spent the first seven years of his adult life. Erasmus was unhappy during this period, largely because the monks discouraged his classical studies. In 1492 he left to work for the Bishop of Cambrai, moving to study in Paris three years later. During this period Erasmus began teaching in order to finance his own studies of Latin. He also published his *Antibarbarorum Liber* ("The Book of Antibarbarians"), in which he stressed the importance of the study of classical texts.

From 1499 onward Erasmus moved restlessly from city to city across Europe, studying and teaching, sponsored by various wealthy patrons. He made several trips to England, where he learned Greek and met many

Above: A portrait of Erasmus painted by the great artist Hans Holbein.

IN PRAISE OF FOLLY

Erasmus's *In Praise of Folly* is a masterpiece. It was begun during a visit with his friend Thomas More, and its Latin title, *Moriae encomium*, is a pun on More's name. A biting satire, the work's targets include personal vanity and political and church corruption. Monks, priests, cardinals, and popes are all ridiculed for their hypocrisy and greed. Had the author been unknown, he would have been charged with heresy; but Erasmus had powerful friends, and the book was a remarkable success. Translated into a dozen languages, it inspired countless satirical writers in the centuries to come. The work has often been described as the world's first bestseller.

Below: The title page from Erasmus's book Colloquia, *a collection of witty dialogues attacking superstition and church corruption.*

influential people, including the politician Thomas More and the religious thinker John Colet. In 1500 he made his literary reputation with the publication of *Adagia* ("Proverbs"), a collection of Latin and Greek proverbs. It proved to be a source of inspiration for many European writers. In 1509 Erasmus moved from Italy to England at the invitation of King Henry VIII, becoming professor of Greek and divinity at Cambridge University.

After writing the popular satire *In Praise of Folly* in 1511, Erasmus then went on to produce a more accurate version of the Greek New Testament, later translating it into Latin (1516). By returning to the original sources, he hoped to bring Christians closer to the true spirit of Christ's teachings. Although Erasmus remained a devout Catholic priest, his work influenced many religious reformers of the time, including Martin Luther.

THE REFORMATION

In 1517 Erasmus's life was thrown into turmoil by events in Germany after the monk Martin Luther pinned a list of 95 theses (articles) to the door of the church in Wittenberg. These theses

Although Erasmus was fiercely critical of the church, he remained a firm believer in church unity

attacked the wealth and corrupt nature of the Catholic church. Calls for reform soon turned to demands for a separate reformed church after Luther's teachings were condemned at a special trial before the Diet of Worms in 1521.

During this period of conflict within the church Erasmus tried to maintain a neutral position. Since he shared many of Luther's views on church corruption, many traditionalists accused Erasmus of encouraging Luther to break from Rome. However, although he was fiercely critical of many aspects of the church, Erasmus

Above: One of the colleges of Cambridge University, England, where Erasmus was appointed professor of Greek and divinity in 1509.

never supported Luther's split. Erasmus was a firm believer in the unity of the church and also disagreed with Luther on the issue of human free will, which Luther did not believe in. Erasmus made many pleas for tolerance and understanding, but they were ignored by both sides.

ATTACK ON CORRUPTION

Despite the conflict, Erasmus continued to produce controversial pieces of work. In 1522 he wrote his second bestseller, *Colloquia* ("Dialogues"). Originally intended to promote conversational Latin as the common language of Europe, it ended up attacking superstition and church corruption through a series of humorous dialogues. It made such an impact that the Holy Roman emperor Charles V ordered the execution of any teacher found using it in the classroom.

Erasmus's belief in the power of education was the central theme of his next great work, *De pueris instituendis* ("On the Education of Boys"), published in 1529. Erasmus believed that if rulers received a thorough education, then they were less likely to engage in bloody and needless wars. He was also a strong supporter of the education of women. Many of his later works were dedicated to female patrons.

Erasmus died in Basel in 1536. Eight years after his death his enemies finally caught up with him when he was excommunicated by the Spanish Inquisition, and his works were briefly banned. Today Erasmus is thought of as one of the greatest intellectuals of the Renaissance. He left behind a huge body of work, including more than 1,500 letters. Although he lived in an age of bitter religious conflict, he always spoke out in favor of tolerance.

Este Family

Although it lay between stronger neighbors—Venice and Florence—the Italian city of Ferrara was one of the most stable states of the Renaissance period. A generally peaceful rule by the Este dynasty enabled the region and its inhabitants to prosper. Some of the Renaissance's greatest artists thrived under Este patronage.

The Este family reigned in Ferrara from 1264, when Obizzo II d'Este (ruled 1264–1293) was elected perpetual lord of the city. Ferrara was officially under the authority of the pope, and for many years there was considerable tension between the Este family and whichever pope was in office at the time.

LORDS OF THE CITY

In 1391, however, Obizzo's descendant Alberto V d'Este (ruled 1388–1393) convinced the pope to allow the Este family to rule the city-state as vicars, or representatives of the Catholic church. From Alberto's time the Este effectively held absolute power in Ferrara until the city returned to papal rule in 1598. Power was passed to the male heirs, and

Above: This painting of life at the Ferrara court shows the 16th-century poet Torquato Tasso reading his epic poem Jerusalem Liberated *to members of the Este family.*

the ruler was given the title of *signore*, or lord. The *signore* would fill important political offices either with other members of the Este family or with their associates.

GREAT STABILITY

Ferrara's unique political arrangement worked to the benefit of the citizens as well as the Este family, since papal authority gave the *signore* a degree of legitimacy that few other Italian Renaissance rulers possessed. As a result, Ferrara enjoyed far greater stability than most other cities in Italy and managed to resist any attempts by its neighbors to conquer it. Most of the conflicts that did emerge in Ferrara were between various members of the Este family themselves.

Below: The Castello Estense in Ferrara, home to the Este family for centuries. The castle was originally built in the 14th century for Nicolò II.

Ferrara flourished over the course of the 15th century. Alberto's son Nicolò III (ruled 1393–1441) was an exceptionally able politician who greatly strengthened the family's grip on power in the city. He also played an active role in the politics of Italy as a whole. His successor Leonello (ruled 1441–1450) earned a considerable reputation as a patron of the arts. His interest in humanism led him to commission works from such great artists as Pisanello, Mantegna, van der Weyden, and Jacopo Bellini.

Este power reached its high point during the rule of Leonello's brother Borso (ruled 1450–1471). In 1452 Borso was named duke of Modena and Reggio by the emperor Frederick III, and the pope gave him the title of duke of Ferrara in 1471. Like his brother Leonello, Borso was an extremely enthusiastic patron of the arts. During his reign a unique Ferrarese school of painting emerged, led by the artists Francesco del Cossa and Cosmè Tura, who is considered the founder of Ferrarese painting.

IMPORTANT ALLIANCES

Borso was succeeded by his half-brother Ercole I (ruled 1471–1505). Ercole's reign marked a turbulent period in Ferrara's history. Ercole lost a large amount of the city's territory in a war with the powerful city-state of Venice, which had an important ally in Pope Sixtus IV.

In order to strengthen his position, Ercole made a series of important alliances through marriage. His three daughters married leading members of the ruling families of Milan, Mantua, and Bologna. His son Alfonso, meanwhile, married first Anna Sforza of Milan and then Lucrezia Borgia, daughter of Pope Alexander VI.

ISABELLA D'ESTE

Renaissance Italy was a world dominated by men. One woman who made a considerable impact, however, was the princess Isabella d'Este (1474–1539). Daughter of Duke Ercole I of Ferrara and Eleonora of Aragon, Isabella grew up surrounded by art and culture. By the age of 16 she could speak Greek and Latin as well as play the lute, sing, and dance. In 1490 she married Francesco Gonzaga II, the marquis of Mantua, and began a career that would earn her the title "the First Lady of the Renaissance."

Isabella often governed Mantua in Francesco's absence and ruled independently for several years after her husband's death. She had a reputation for fairness and political shrewdness, much evidence of which can be found in the thousands of letters and other correspondence she left behind. Her patronage of the arts was as generous as that of the rest of the Este family. Isabella was the subject of portraits by such noted painters as Cosmè Tura, Titian, and Leonardo da Vinci. Her extensive collection of art included works by Raphael, Correggio, Dosso Dossi, Titian, and Michelangelo.

Right: A portrait of Isabella d'Este by the Venetian artist Gian Francesco Caroto.

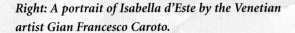

Despite these political distractions, Ercole continued his family's tradition of supporting the arts. In particular, he sponsored a major redevelopment project carried out largely by the architect Biagio Rossetti. The project earned Ferrara the distinction of being the first planned Renaissance city and included an expansion of the city walls, the construction of many new buildings, and the enlargement of the cathedral.

CONFLICTS WITH ROME

Over the course of the 16th century the dukes of Ferrara increasingly came into conflict with the pope. Alfonso I (ruled 1505–1534) was excommunicated by Pope Julius II because of his close political ties with France. Alfonso's son Ercole II (ruled 1534–1559) proved equally unpopular with Rome, mainly because his wife Renée was a strong supporter of Martin Luther. Against her husband's wishes she allowed the court at Ferrara to become a meeting place for Protestant intellectuals.

The Este family's control of Ferrara ended with the death of Alfonso II (ruled 1559–1598). Despite being married three times, Alfonso left no legitimate children. He tried to pass control of the city to his cousin, but Pope Clement VII refused to recognize the deal. After over 300 years of Este rule Ferrara passed back into the hands of the papacy.

SEE ALSO

♦ Alexander VI
♦ Borgia Family
♦ City-States
♦ Courts and Court Culture
♦ Florence
♦ Gonzaga Family
♦ Mantegna
♦ Padua
♦ Palaces and Villas
♦ Papacy
♦ Papal States
♦ Patronage
♦ Sforza Family
♦ Titian
♦ Venice

Exploration

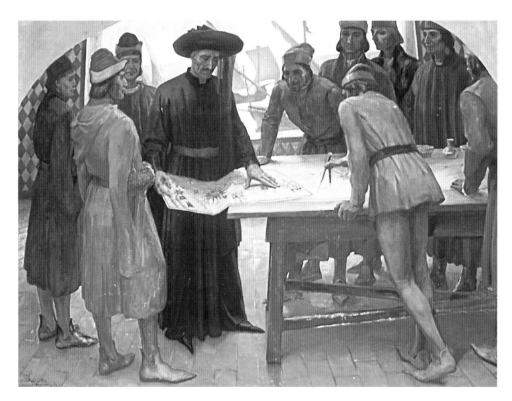

Left: Henry the Navigator studying a map, surrounded by his young sea captains. Henry sponsored sea expeditions to explore south along the west African coast, and by the time he died in 1460 his ships had reached as far as Cape Palmas.

The 15th century was a period of intense exploration, as hardy adventurers braved tumultuous oceans in tiny vessels in attempts to find new lands and new sea routes to the Spice Islands of the East. Their discoveries marked a turning point in European history, shifting the focus of trade from the Mediterranean to the Atlantic, opening up new lands for settlement, and transforming Europe's view of the world.

The spice trade was controlled by Islam and the Ottoman Turks in the East, and Venice was the dominant port for the spices to enter Europe. If any European power could discover an alternative route to the Spice Islands, it would gain a supreme trading advantage.

Portugal played a pioneering role. Prince Henry (1394–1460), the younger son of John I of Portugal, sponsored the first expeditions along the west African coast, earning himself the title "Henry the Navigator." Henry hoped to set up links with Africa south of the Sahara Desert and with Asia to trade in slaves, gold, and spices. He also hoped to forge an anti-Islamic alliance with the legendary African Christian king, Prester John.

For sailors to venture beyond the known limits of the north African coast, it was necessary to develop better ships and navigational techniques. Henry set up the first maritime academy in Europe at Sagres, his headquarters in Portugal. There sailors and navigators studied astronomy and

THE TREATY OF TORDESILLAS

Following the discovery of the New World in 1492, Pope Alexander VI negotiated a treaty between Spain and Portugal that divided the entire non-Christian world in two along an imaginary north–south line in the mid-Atlantic, 300 miles (480km) west of the Cape Verde Islands. All new lands discovered west of the line would belong to Spain; everything to the east would belong to Portugal. However, Portuguese dissatisfaction with these terms led in 1494 to a renegotiated treaty, with the demarcation line moved a further 800 miles (1,280km) west.

This meant that Spain claimed sovereignty over the recently discovered New World. Portugal claimed everything to the east, which included not only the lucrative trading route to the east via Africa, but also Brazil, which was discovered by Pedro Cabral in 1500.

Below: Vasco da Gama being received in Calicut by the local Hindu ruler in May 1498.

the winds and the currents of the sea, knowledge that was vital for the exploration of the African coastline. While sailors could follow the coast southward, the prevailing winds meant they had to return out of sight of land.

Henry's first expeditions reached the islands of Madeira in 1419 and the Azores in 1427, and they became Portugal's first colonies. Little by little, Henry's navigators pushed their way down the African coast, reaching Cape Bojador in 1434, Cape Verde (Africa's most westerly point) in 1444, and Cape Palmas in 1460. The introduction of a new type of ship, the caravel, in 1440 made the voyages safer and faster (see box on page 67).

By the time Henry died in 1460, his mariners had charted 1,500 miles (2,400km) of African coastline, as far as present-day Sierra Leone, but they had still many challenges to face. In 1471 Portuguese sailors crossed the Doldrums (a windless region around the equator), reaching the Congo in 1482 and Namibia in 1486.

BARTHOLOMEU DIAS

The great breakthrough was made by Bartholomeu Dias (about 1450–1500). In August 1487 he left Lisbon with orders to find Africa's southern tip. Reaching Namibia in January 1488, he was driven out of sight of land by violent storms for a whole month. When he saw land again, he was sailing northward, having rounded the tip of Africa—later named the Cape of Good

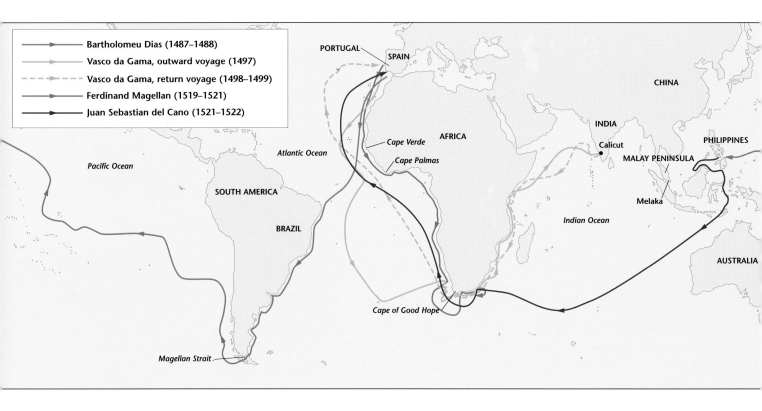

Legend:
- Bartholomeu Dias (1487–1488)
- Vasco da Gama, outward voyage (1497)
- Vasco da Gama, return voyage (1498–1499)
- Ferdinand Magellan (1519–1521)
- Juan Sebastian del Cano (1521–1522)

Above: A map showing the voyages of the great explorers who discovered new sea routes to Asia.

Hope—without seeing it. He had reached the Indian Ocean, but his men were so exhausted that they forced him to return home.

Dias's discovery proved that an eastward route to the Indies did exist. This was in flat contradiction to the map of the world used at the time, which was based on a map drawn by the ancient Greek astronomer Ptolemy around 200 A.D. and showed a landlocked Indian Ocean.

VASCO DA GAMA

It was nine years before anyone followed up Dias's discovery. In July 1497 Vasco da Gama (about 1460–1524) left Lisbon with four ships and instructions to reach Calicut—an important trading center on the west coast of India. Rounding the cape, da Gama sailed up the uncharted east coast of Africa, putting in at several ports on the way and having some hair-raising adventures. Eventually he crossed the Indian Ocean with the help of an Indian navigator—Indian and Arab traders had been sailing across the Indian Ocean for centuries.

In May 1498 da Gama reached Calicut, but failed to secure a trading agreement with the local Hindu ruler. However, following his triumphant return to Portugal in 1499, a larger expedition was sent out under Pedro Cabral (1467–1520). This expedition was blown so far off course that it landed in Brazil, claiming it for Portugal. Back on course, Cabral reached Calicut, where he set up a settlement. He returned to Portugal with a rich cargo of spices. He was followed by other pioneering navigators, and by 1511 Portugal controlled Melaka on the Malay peninsula—at the time the center of the spice trade—and ports in the Indian Ocean, making it the most important sea-trading nation in the world.

Meanwhile another adventurer had been pursuing the westward route to the Indies. Christopher Columbus

Left: A 19th-century print showing Christopher Columbus landing in the Bahamas on his first pioneering voyage to the New World. Columbus was convinced that he had found a new sea route to Asia.

Below: The four voyages of Christopher Columbus. After his first voyage in 1492 Columbus explored the whole Caribbean region over a period of 12 years.

(1451–1506) was born in Genoa, Italy, and went to sea at an early age. In the 1470s he started to plot a westward route to Asia across the Atlantic. Like many other people at that time, Columbus knew the earth was round, but he believed it to be much smaller than it really is.

SAILING WEST TO THE EAST

Columbus's plan was to sail west for China, making his first landfall on Cipangu (Japan), off the Chinese coast. But he hugely underestimated the distances involved, calculating Cipangu to be only 2,750 miles (4,400km) distant from Spain—the real distance is over 11,000 miles (17,600km).

In 1484 Columbus presented his plans to King John II of Portugal, who refused to sponsor an expedition. The following year Columbus moved to Spain and for six years continually petitioned the Spanish king and queen, Ferdinand and Isabella, for their support. In January 1492 he finally received approval for his plans. On August 3 Columbus set sail from Palos

in southwest Spain with three ships—the *Santa Maria*, the *Niña*, and the *Pinta*—and 120 crew. Using the trade winds, he sailed from the Canary Islands straight across the Atlantic, making landfall in the Bahamas on

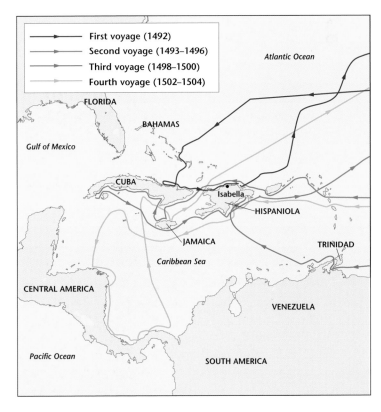

First voyage (1492)	
Second voyage (1493–1496)	
Third voyage (1498–1500)	
Fourth voyage (1502–1504)	

Atlantic Ocean

FLORIDA

BAHAMAS

Gulf of Mexico

CUBA

Isabella

HISPANIOLA

JAMAICA

TRINIDAD

Caribbean Sea

CENTRAL AMERICA

VENEZUELA

Pacific Ocean

SOUTH AMERICA

October 12. Columbus claimed the island for Spain, naming it San Salvador. He sailed on to Cuba and another island he named Hispaniola (now Haiti and the Dominican Republic). He returned to Spain convinced he had found a route to Asia.

Columbus made three more voyages across the Atlantic. On his second voyage (1493–1496) he explored the Caribbean islands and established a colony called Isabella on Hispaniola. On his third voyage (1498–1500) he reached Trinidad and Venezuela, while on the final one (1502–1504) he navigated along the Gulf of Mexico trying to find a passage to India.

EXOTIC PRESENTS

When Columbus returned to Spain in March 1493 after his first voyage, he presented the king and queen with parrots, gold, and six captive "Indians," so-called because Columbus believed he had returned from Asia. It was only when he landed on Venezuela on the South American mainland in 1498 that he realized he had found, as he recorded, a "very large continent, which until now has remained unknown." Despite this, he continued to insist publicly that he had reached Asia.

After four voyages Spain had nothing to show for its efforts and had been beaten by Portugal to the prize of finding a sea route to the Indies. Following the failure of his final voyage, Columbus was stripped of his titles and died 18 months later. As a last indignity, a new map was published naming the new continent "America"

Above: A 16th-century portrait of the Portuguese explorer Ferdinand Magellan, who was the first mariner to sail from Europe to the East Indies via the tip of South America and the Pacific Ocean.

after the Italian navigator Amerigo Vespucci, who had published a biased account of his own "discovery" of a new world.

The European discovery of the New World had a profound effect on the peoples of Europe. It opened up a whole new continent for conquest and colonization, and the vast amounts of gold and silver that were shipped over from its new empire would turn Spain into the West's first superpower. The New World also introduced Europeans to some strange new foods—corn (maize) and potatoes.

FERDINAND MAGELLAN

The prize of reaching Asia by a westward route fell to Ferdinand Magellan (1480–1521), the last great Portuguese navigator. Following a distinguished naval career in the Indian Ocean, Magellan renounced his nationality after disagreements with the Portuguese king and offered his services to Spain instead.

He convinced the Spanish king Charles I—later the Holy Roman emperor Charles V—that he knew of a secret passage through the American continent through which he could reach the Spice Islands of the Indies. He also hoped that by sailing west he could claim that the Spice Islands lay west of the line of demarcation set by the Treaty of Tordesillas (see box on page 63) and therefore belonged to Spain.

Magellan finally left Seville in September 1519 in command of five ships. Reaching the South American coast, he found that his secret passage was a huge river mouth—the Rio de

Plata in Argentina—so he systematically explored every inlet and bay along the coast in a vain attempt to locate the vital passage.

By April, with nothing to show for his efforts, Magellan found himself suppressing a mutiny of his Spanish captains, who resented taking orders from a Portuguese. Finally, in October 1520 Magellan found a strait, now named after him, at the tip of South America. It was narrow and dangerous, and it took the ships a month to sail through it. The gentle winds on the other side inspired Magellan to name the new ocean the Pacific.

THE GREAT PACIFIC

The Pacific was considerably larger than Magellan had imagined, and his ships sailed for over two months with no sight of land. His crew suffered from thirst, starvation, and scurvy, a disease caused by the lack of fresh fruit and vegetables, before they finally reached the island of Guam in March 1521.

Magellan then sailed on to Cebu in the Philippines, which he recognized from the time when he had served in the Indian Ocean. There, after having successfully navigated 12,600 miles (20,200km) across the Pacific Ocean and reaching his goal, he was killed in April in a skirmish with a local chief. One of Magellan's ships—the *Victoria*, captained by Juan Sebastian del Cano—managed to return to Spain in September 1522, having sailed all the way around the world. Of the original 270 men with whom Magellan set out only 17 survived.

Magellan's momentous voyage provided the final pieces of the jigsaw that made up the European view of the world. It was much larger than had been thought, all the oceans were connected, and the East and West Indies were on opposite sides of the world.

SEE ALSO
◆ Africa
◆ Americas
◆ Navigation
◆ Portugal
◆ Ships
◆ Spain
◆ Trade

THE CARAVEL

One reason why the Portuguese were such successful explorers was the caravel, a special type of ship built specifically for exploration rather than trade. Its design, which was a closely guarded secret, was perfected by Portuguese shipbuilders during the early 15th century to spearhead a series of exploratory voyages along the west African coast sponsored by Henry the Navigator.

Using a blend of European shipbuilding skills and Arab sail technology, the caravel combined a small, compact body 60–100 ft (18–30m) long with two or three masts. They carried a lateen sail—a triangular sail used on Arab dhows in the Indian Ocean—on the rear mast and square sails on the other masts. The lateen's leading edge hung down, rather than across, the mast so that it could be pointed forward, allowing the ship to sail into the wind. This gave the caravel extra speed and maneuverability, making it ideal for exploring the coastline at close quarters.

Above: A painting of two of Columbus's ships, both caravels. The lateen (triangular) sail at the stern of the caravel helped it sail into the wind.

Timeline

♦ **1305** Giotto begins work on frescoes for the Arena Chapel, Padua—he is often considered the father of Renaissance art.

♦ **1321** Dante publishes the *Divine Comedy*, which has a great influence on later writers.

♦ **1327** Petrarch begins writing the sonnets known as the *Canzoniere*.

♦ **1337** The start of the Hundred Years' War between England and France.

♦ **1353** Boccaccio writes the *Decameron*, an influential collection of 100 short stories.

♦ **1368** The Ming dynasty comes to power in China.

♦ **1377** Pope Gregory XI moves the papacy back to Rome from Avignon, where it has been based since 1309.

♦ **1378** The Great Schism begins: two popes, Urban VI and Clement VII, both lay claim to the papacy.

♦ **1378** English theologian John Wycliffe criticizes the practices of the Roman Catholic church.

♦ **1380** Ivan I of Muscovy defeats the army of the Mongol Golden Horde at the battle of Kulikovo.

♦ **1389** The Ottomans defeat the Serbs at the battle of Kosovo, beginning a new phase of Ottoman expansion.

♦ **1397** Sigismund of Hungary is defeated by the Ottoman Turks at the battle of Nicopolis.

♦ **1397** Queen Margaret of Denmark unites Denmark, Sweden, and Norway under the Union of Kalmar.

♦ **1398** The Mongol leader Tamerlane invades India.

♦ **1399** Henry Bolingbroke becomes Henry IV of England.

♦ **1400** English writer Geoffrey Chaucer dies, leaving his *Canterbury Tales* unfinished.

♦ **1403** In Italy the sculptor Ghiberti wins a competition to design a new set of bronze doors for Florence Cathedral.

♦ **c.1402** The Bohemian preacher Jan Hus begins to attack the corruption of the church.

♦ **1405** The Chinese admiral Cheng Ho commands the first of seven expeditions to the Indian Ocean and East Africa.

♦ **1415** Jan Hus is summoned to the Council of Constance and condemned to death.

♦ **1415** Henry V leads the English to victory against the French at the battle of Agincourt.

♦ **c.1415** Florentine sculptor Donatello produces his sculpture *Saint George*.

♦ **1416** Venice defeats the Ottoman fleet at the battle of Gallipoli, but does not check the Ottoman advance.

♦ **1417** The Council of Constance elects Martin V pope, ending the Great Schism.

♦ **1418** Brunelleschi designs the dome of Florence Cathedral.

♦ **1420** Pope Martin V returns the papacy to Rome, bringing peace and order to the city.

♦ **c.1420** Prince Henry of Portugal founds a school of navigation at Sagres, beginning a great age of Portuguese exploration.

♦ **1422** Charles VI of France dies, leaving his throne to the English king Henry VI. Charles VI's son also claims the throne.

♦ **c.1425** Florentine artist Masaccio paints the *Holy Trinity*, the first painting to use the new science of perspective.

♦ **1429** Joan of Arc leads the French to victory at Orléans; Charles VII is crowned king of France in Reims Cathedral.

♦ **1431** The English burn Joan of Arc at the stake for heresy.

♦ **1433** Sigismund of Luxembourg becomes Holy Roman emperor.

♦ **1434** Cosimo de Medici comes to power in Florence.

♦ **1434** The Flemish artist Jan van Eyck paints the *Arnolfini Marriage* using the newly developed medium of oil paint.

♦ **1439** The Council of Florence proclaims the reunion of the Western and Orthodox churches.

♦ **c.1440** Donatello completes his statue of David—the first life-size bronze sculpture since antiquity.

♦ **1443** Federigo da Montefeltro becomes ruler of Urbino.

♦ **1447** The Milanese people declare their city a republic.

♦ **1450** The condottiere Francesco Sforza seizes control of Milan.

♦ **1450** Fra Angelico paints *The Annunciation* for the monastery of San Marco in Florence.

♦ **1453** Constantinople, capital of the Byzantine Empire, falls to the Ottomans and becomes the capital of the Muslim Empire.

♦ **1453** The French defeat the English at the battle of Castillon, ending the Hundred Years' War.

♦ **1454–1456** Venice, Milan, Florence, Naples, and the papacy form the Italian League to maintain peace in Italy.

♦ **1455** The start of the Wars of the Roses between the Houses of York and Lancaster in England.

♦ **c.1455** The German Johannes Gutenberg develops the first printing press using movable type.

♦ **1456** The Florentine painter Uccello begins work on the *Battle of San Romano*.

♦ **1461** The House of York wins the Wars of the Roses; Edward IV becomes king of England.

♦ **1461** Sonni Ali becomes king of the Songhai Empire in Africa.

♦ **1462** Marsilio Ficino founds the Platonic Academy of Florence—the birthplace of Renaissance Neoplatonism.

♦ **1463** War breaks out between Venice and the Ottoman Empire.

♦ **1465** The Italian painter Mantegna begins work on the Camera degli Sposi in Mantua.

♦ **1467** Civil war breaks out in Japan, lasting for over a century.

♦ **1469** Lorenzo the Magnificent, grandson of Cosimo de Medici, comes to power in Florence.

♦ **1469** The marriage of Isabella I of Castile and Ferdinand V of Aragon unites the two kingdoms.

♦ **1470** The Florentine sculptor Verrocchio completes his *David*.

♦ **1476** William Caxton establishes the first English printing press at Westminster, near London.

♦ **1477** Pope Sixtus IV begins building the Sistine Chapel.

♦ **c.1477** Florentine painter Sandro Botticelli paints the *Primavera*, one of the first large-scale mythological paintings of the Renaissance.

♦ **1478** The Spanish Inquisition is founded in Spain.

♦ **1480** The Ottoman fleet destroys the port of Otranto in south Italy.

♦ **1485** Henry Tudor becomes Henry VII of England—the start of the Tudor dynasty.

♦ **1486** *The Witches' Hammer* is published, a handbook on how to hunt down witches.

♦ **1488** Portuguese navigator Bartholomeu Dias reaches the Cape of Good Hope.

♦ **1491** Missionaries convert King Nzina Nkowu of the Congo to Christianity.

♦ **1492** The Spanish monarchs conquer Granada, the last Moorish territory in Spain.

♦ **1492** Christopher Columbus lands in the Bahamas, claiming the territory for Spain.

♦ **1492** Henry VII of England renounces all English claims to the French throne.

♦ **1493** The Hapsburg Maximilian becomes Holy Roman emperor.

♦ **1494** Charles VIII of France invades Italy, beginning four decades of Italian wars.

♦ **1494** In Italy Savonarola comes to power in Florence.

♦ **1494** The Treaty of Tordesillas divides the non-Christian world between Spain and Portugal.

♦ **1495** Leonardo da Vinci begins work on *The Last Supper* .

♦ **1495** Spain forms a Holy League with the Holy Roman emperor and expels the French from Naples.

♦ **1498** Portuguese navigator Vasco da Gama reaches Calicut, India.

♦ **1498** German artist Dürer creates the *Apocalypse* woodcuts.

♦ **1500** Portuguese navigator Pedro Cabral discovers Brazil.

♦ **c.1500–1510** Dutch painter Hieronymus Bosch paints *The Garden of Earthly Delights*.

♦ **c.1502** Italian architect Donato Bramante designs the Tempietto Church in Rome.

♦ **1503** Leonardo da Vinci begins painting the *Mona Lisa*.

♦ **1504** Michelangelo finishes his statue of David, widely seen as a symbol of Florence.

♦ **c.1505** Venetian artist Giorgione paints *The Tempest*.

♦ **1506** The Italian architect Donato Bramante begins work on rebuilding Saint Peter's, Rome.

♦ **1508** Michelangelo begins work on the ceiling of the Sistine Chapel in the Vatican.

♦ **1509** Henry VIII ascends the throne of England.

♦ **1509** The League of Cambrai defeats Venice at the battle of Agnadello.

♦ **1510–1511** Raphael paints *The School of Athens* in the Vatican.

♦ **1511** The French are defeated at the battle of Ravenna in Italy and are forced to retreat over the Alps.

♦ **1513** Giovanni de Medici becomes Pope Leo X.

♦ **1515** Thomas Wolsey becomes lord chancellor of England.

♦ **1515** Francis I becomes king of France. He invades Italy and captures Milan.

♦ **c.1515** German artist Grünewald paints the *Isenheim Altarpiece.*

♦ **1516** Charles, grandson of the emperor Maximilian I, inherits the Spanish throne as Charles I.

♦ **1516** Thomas More publishes his political satire *Utopia.*

♦ **1516** Dutch humanist Erasmus publishes a more accurate version of the Greek New Testament.

♦ **1517** Martin Luther pins his 95 theses on the door of the castle church in Wittenburg.

♦ **1519** Charles I of Spain becomes Holy Roman emperor Charles V.

♦ **1519–1521** Hernán Cortés conquers Mexico for Spain.

♦ **1520** Henry VIII of England and Francis I of France meet at the Field of the Cloth of Gold to sign a treaty of friendship.

♦ **1520** Portuguese navigator Ferdinand Magellan discovers a route to the Indies around the tip of South America.

♦ **1520** Süleyman the Magnificent becomes ruler of the Ottoman Empire, which now dominates the eastern Mediterranean.

♦ **1520–1523** Titian paints *Bacchus and Ariadne* for Alfonso d'Este.

♦ **1521** Pope Leo X excommuicates Martin Luther.

♦ **1521** The emperor Charles V attacks France, beginning a long period of European war.

♦ **1522** Ferdinand Magellan's ship the *Victoria* is the first to sail around the world.

♦ **1523–1525** Huldrych Zwingli sets up a Protestant church at Zurich in Switzerland.

♦ **1525** In Germany the Peasants' Revolt is crushed, and its leader, Thomas Münzer, is executed.

♦ **1525** The emperor Charles V defeats the French at the battle of Pavia and takes Francis I prisoner.

♦ **1525** William Tyndale translates the New Testament into English.

♦ **1526** The Ottoman Süleyman the Magnificent defeats Hungary at the battle of Mohács.

♦ **1526** Muslim Mongol leader Babur invades northern India and establishes the Mogul Empire.

♦ **c.1526** The Italian artist Correggio paints the *Assumption of the Virgin* in Parma Cathedral.

♦ **1527** Charles V's armies overrun Italy and sack Rome.

♦ **1527–1530** Gustavus I founds a Lutheran state church in Sweden.

♦ **1528** Italian poet and humanist Baldassare Castiglione publishes *The Courtier.*

♦ **1529** The Ottoman Süleyman the Magnificent lays siege to Vienna, but eventually retreats.

♦ **1530** The Catholic church issues the "Confutation," attacking Luther and Protestantism.

♦ **1531** The Protestant princes of Germany form the Schmalkaldic League.

♦ **1531–1532** Francisco Pizarro conquers Peru for Spain.

♦ **1532** Machiavelli's *The Prince* is published after his death.

♦ **1533** Henry VIII of England rejects the authority of the pope and marries Anne Boleyn.

♦ **1533** Anabaptists take over the city of Münster in Germany.

♦ **1533** Christian III of Denmark founds the Lutheran church of Denmark.

♦ **1534** Paul III becomes pope and encourages the growth of new religious orders such as the Jesuits.

♦ **1534** Luther publishes his German translation of the Bible.

♦ **1534** The Act of Supremacy declares Henry VIII supreme head of the Church of England.

♦ **c.1535** Parmigianino paints the mannerist masterpiece *Madonna of the Long Neck.*

♦ **1535–1536** The Swiss city of Geneva becomes Protestant and expels the Catholic clergy.

♦ **1536** Calvin publishes *Institutes of the Christian Religion*, which sets out his idea of predestination.

♦ **1536** Pope Paul III sets up a reform commission to examine the state of the Catholic church.

♦ **1537** Hans Holbein is appointed court painter to Henry VIII of England.

♦ **1539** Italian painter Bronzino begins working for Cosimo de Medici the Younger in Florence.

♦ **1539** Ignatius de Loyola founds the Society of Jesus (the Jesuits).

♦ **1541** John Calvin sets up a model Christian city in Geneva.

♦ **1543** Andreas Vesalius publishes *On the Structure of the Human Body*, a handbook of anatomy based on dissections.

♦ **1543** Polish astronomer Copernicus's *On the Revolutions of the Heavenly Spheres* proposes a sun-centered universe.

♦ **1544** Charles V and Francis I of France sign the Truce of Crespy.

♦ **1545** Pope Paul III organizes the Council of Trent to counter the threat of Protestantism.

♦ **1545** Spanish explorers find huge deposits of silver in the Andes Mountains of Peru.

♦ **1547** Charles V defeats the Protestant Schmalkaldic League at the Battle of Mühlberg.

♦ **1547** Ivan IV "the Terrible" declares himself czar of Russia.

♦ **1548** Titian paints the equestrian portrait *Charles V after the Battle of Mühlberg.*

♦ **1548** Tintoretto paints *Saint Mark Rescuing the Slave.*

♦ **1550** Italian Georgio Vasari publishes his *Lives of the Artists.*

♦ **1553** Mary I of England restores the Catholic church.

♦ **1554** Work begins on the Cathedral of Saint Basil in Red Square, Moscow.

♦ **1555** At the Peace of Augsburg Charles V allows the German princes to determine their subjects' religion.

♦ **1556** Ivan IV defeats the last Mongol khanates. Muscovy now dominates the Volga region.

♦ **1556** Philip II becomes king of Spain.

♦ **1559** Elizabeth I of England restores the Protestant church.

♦ **1562** The Wars of Religion break out in France.

♦ **1565** Flemish artist Pieter Bruegel the Elder paints *Hunters in the Snow.*

♦ **1565** Italian architect Palladio designs the Villa Rotunda, near Vicenza.

♦ **1566** The Dutch revolt against the Spanish over the loss of political and religious freedoms:

Philip II of Spain sends 10,000 troops under the duke of Alba to suppress the revolt.

♦ **1569** Flemish cartographer Mercator produces a world map using a new projection.

♦ **1571** Philip II of Spain and an allied European force defeat the Ottomans at the battle of Lepanto.

♦ **1572** In Paris, France, a Catholic mob murders thousands of Huguenots in the Saint Bartholomew's Day Massacre.

♦ **1572** Danish astronomer Tycho Brahe sees a new star.

♦ **1573** Venetian artist Veronese paints the *Feast of the House of Levi.*

♦ **1579** The seven northern provinces of the Netherlands form the Union of Utrecht.

♦ **1580** Giambologna creates his mannerist masterpiece *Flying Mercury.*

♦ **1585** Henry III of France bans Protestantism in France; civil war breaks out again in the War of the Three Henrys.

♦ **1586** El Greco, a Greek artist active in Spain, paints the *Burial of Count Orgaz.*

♦ **1587** Mary, Queen of Scots, is executed by Elizabeth I of England.

♦ **c.1587** Nicholas Hilliard paints the miniature *Young Man among Roses.*

♦ **1588** Philip II of Spain launches his great Armada against England —but the fleet is destroyed.

♦ **1589** Henry of Navarre becomes king of France as Henry IV.

♦ **1592–1594** Tintoretto paints *The Last Supper.*

♦ **1596** Edmund Spencer publishes the *Faerie Queene*, glorifying Elizabeth I as "Gloriana."

♦ **1598** Henry IV of France grants Huguenots and Catholics equal political rights.

♦ **1598** In England the Globe Theater is built on London's south bank; it stages many of Shakespeare's plays.

♦ **1600–1601** Caravaggio paints *The Crucifixion of Saint Peter*, an early masterpiece of baroque art.

♦ **1603** Elizabeth I of England dies and is succeeded by James I, son of Mary, Queen of Scots.

♦ **1610** Galileo's *The Starry Messenger* supports the sun-centered model of the universe.

♦ **1620** The Italian painter Artemisia Gentileschi paints *Judith and Holofernes.*

Glossary

A.D. The letters A.D. stand for the Latin Anno Domini, which means "in the year of our Lord." Dates with these letters written after them are measured forward from the year Christ was born.

Altarpiece A painting or sculpture placed behind an altar in a church.

Apprentice Someone legally bound to a craftsman for a number of years in order to learn a craft.

B.C. Short for "Before Christ." Dates with these letters after them are measured backward from the year of Christ's birth.

Branding Marking an animal or a person with a hot iron to show ownership.

Bureaucracy A system of government that relies on a body of officials and usually involves much paperwork and many regulations.

Chalice A drinking cup, often made of gold or silver, that is used in the church communion service.

Classical A term used to describe the civilizations of ancient Greece and Rome, and any later art and architecture based on ancient Greek and Roman examples.

Condottiere A mercenary soldier, that is, a soldier who will fight for any employer in return for money.

Connoisseur An expert in a particular fine art or in a matter of taste.

Curfew A regulation banning people from the streets, usually after dark.

Envoy Someone sent abroad to represent the government.

Excommunicate To ban someone from taking part in the rites of the church.

Foreshortening A technique used by artists in their pictures to recreate the appearance of objects when seen from a particular angle. It involves shortening some measurements, according to the laws of perspective (see below), to make it look as if objects are projecting toward or receding away from the picture surface.

Fresco A type of painting that is usually used for decorating walls and ceilings in which colors are painted into wet plaster.

Guild An association that regulated the training and work of professionals, merchants, and craftsmen in the Middle Ages and the Renaissance.

Heresy A belief that is contrary to the accepted teachings of the church.

Heretic Someone whose beliefs contradict those of the church.

Humanism A new way of thinking about human life that characterized the Renaissance. It was based on the study of "humanities"—that is, ancient Greek and Roman texts, history, and philosophy—and stressed the importance of developing rounded, cultured people.

Humanist Someone who adopted humanism, the new way of thinking about human life that characterized the Renaissance.

Hundred Years' War A long-drawn-out war between France and England, lasting from 1337 to 1453. It consisted of a series of campaigns with periods of tense peace in between.

Indulgences Cancelations of punishment for sins. Indulgences were often granted by the church in return for money.

Journeyman A qualified craftsman who has completed his apprenticeship and works for another person on either a specific project or a daily basis.

Laity or lay people Anyone who is not of the clergy.

Majolica A type of pottery made in Spain. It is covered with a white glaze and decorated with brightly colored patterns and scenes.

Mercenary A soldier who will fight for any employer in return for money.

Monstrance A special container made to hold the consecrated bread that is used in the church communion service.

Patron Someone who orders and pays for a work of art.

Patronage The act of ordering and paying for a work of art.

Perspective A technique that allows artists to create the impression of three-dimensional space in their pictures. Near objects are made to appear larger, and distant objects smaller.

Purgatory A place of suffering through which Catholics believe people's souls pass after they have died. The suffering and punishments in purgatory are believed to cleanse people's souls of sin. Purgatory was much feared in the Renaissance.

Relic In the Catholic religion part of the body of a saint or an item associated with them, which is worshiped as holy.

Reliquary A special container used to keep sacred relics in.

Siege A military blockade of a castle or town to force it to surrender, often by cutting off its supplies of food and water.

Simony Buying or selling a church office.

Tempera A type of paint made by mixing pigments (colors) with egg yolk. Tempera was widely used by painters in the Middle Ages and Renaissance.

Theologian Someone who studies religious faith, practice, and experience.

Treason The name given to a subject's act of betrayal of their king or queen.

Treatise A book or long essay about the principles, or rules, of a particular subject.

Vassal A person who is bound to a local lord to whom they owe their loyalty and services.

Vernacular The language of the ordinary people of a country, rather than a literary or formal language like Latin.

Further Reading

Ames-Lewis, Francis. *Drawing in Early Renaissance Italy.* New Haven, CT: Yale University Press, 2000.

Ashby, Ruth. *Elizabethan England.* New York: Benchmark Books, 1999.

Bialostocki, Jan. *The Art of the Renaissance in Eastern Europe: Hungary, Bohemia, Poland.* Ithaca, NY: Cornell University Press, 1976.

Braunmiller, A.R., and Michael Hattaway (editors). *The Cambridge Companion to English Renaissance Drama.* Cambridge, UK: Cambridge University Press, 1990.

Burdett, Lois. *A Child's Portrait of Shakespeare.* Windsor, ON: Black Moss Press, 1995.

Butts, Barbara and Lee Hendrix. *Painting on Light: Drawings and Stained Glass in the Age of Dürer and Holbein.* Los Angeles, CA: Getty Trust Publication, 2001.

Cameron, Euan. *The European Reformation.* Oxford: Oxford University Press, 1995.

Castiglione, Baldassare. *The Book of the Courtier.* New York: W.W. Norton, 2001.

Cole, Alison. *Eyewitness: Renaissance.* New York: DK Publishing, 2000.

Curry, Patrick and Oscar Zarate. *Introducing Machiavelli.* New York: Totem Books, 1996.

Day, Nancy. *Your Travel Guide to Renaissance Europe.* Minneapolis, MN: Runestone Press, 2001.

Dewald, Jonathan. *The European Nobility, 1400–1800.* Cambridge, UK: Cambridge University Press, 1996.

Dürer, Albrecht. *Drawings of Albrecht Dürer.* New York: Dover Publications, 1970.

Dürer, Albrecht. *The Complete Engravings, Etchings and Drypoints of Albrecht Dürer.* New York: Dover Publications, 1973.

Ekserdijian, David. *Correggio.* New Haven, CT: Yale University Press, 1998.

Elton, G.R. *England under the Tudors.* London: Routledge, 1991.

Erasmus, Desiderius. *The Praise of Folly and Other Writings: A New Translation with Critical Commentary.* New York: W.W. Norton, 1989.

Gaeta Bertelà, Giovanna. *Donatello.* New York: Riverside Book Company, 1994.

Henry, John. *Moving Heaven and Earth: Copernicus and the Solar System.* Cambridge, UK: Icon Books, 2001.

Herald, Jacqueline. *Renaissance Dress in Italy 1400–1500.* Atlantic Highlands, NJ: Humanities Press, 1981.

Hibbert, Christopher. *The Virgin Queen: Elizabeth I, Genius of the Golden Age.* Reading, MA: Addison-Wesley Publishing, 1991.

Hintz, Martin. *Poland.* Chicago, IL: Children's Press, 1998.

Hollander, Robert. *Dante: A Life in Works.* New Haven, CT: Yale University Press, 2001.

Howarth, Sarah. *Renaissance People.* Brookfield, CT: Millbrook Press, 1992.

Hutchison, Jane Campbell. *Albrecht Dürer.* Princeton, NJ: Princeton University Press, 1992.

Jones, Martin D.W. *The Counter Reformation: Religion and Society in Early Modern Europe.* Cambridge, UK: Cambridge University Press, 1995.

Kinney, Arthur F. *Renaissance Drama: An Anthology of Plays and Entertainments.* Oxford: Blackwell Publishers, 1999.

Lamb, Charles. *Tales from Shakespeare.* New York: Random House, 1999.

Lewis, R.W.B. *Dante.* New York: Viking Press, 2001.

Martell, Hazel Mary. *The Age of Discovery.* New York: Facts on File, 1993.

McConica, James. *Erasmus.* Oxford: Oxford University Press, 1991.

Morison, Samuel Eliot. *Admiral of the Ocean Sea: A Life of Christopher Columbus.* Boston, MA: Northeastern University Press, 1983.

Morley, Jacqueline. *A Renaissance Town.* New York: Peter Bedrick Books, 1996.

Morrill, J.S. (editor). *The Oxford Illustrated History of Tudor and Stuart Britain.* Oxford: Oxford University Press, 2001.

Parry, J. H. *The Age of Reconnaissance.* Berkeley, CA: University of California Press, 1981.

Pigafetta, Antonio. *Magellan's Voyage: A Narrative of the First Circumnavigation.* New York: Dover Publications, 1994.

Plowden, Alison. *Elizabeth Regina: The Age of Triumph 1588–1603.* New York: Times Books, 1980.

Plowden, Alison. *The House of Tudor.* Stroud, UK: Sutton Publishing, 1999.

Russell, Peter. *Prince Henry "the Navigator": A Life.* New Haven, CT: Yale University Press, 2000.

Scalini, Mario. *Benvenuto Cellini.* New York: Riverside Book Company, 1996.

Skinner, Quentin. *Machiavelli: A Very Short Introduction.* Oxford: Oxford University Press, 2000.

Thomas, Jane Resh. *Behind the Mask: The Life of Queen Elizabeth I.* New York: Clarion Books, 1998.

Weiditz, Christoph. *Authentic Everyday Dress of the Renaissance: All 154 Plates from the "Trachtenbuch."* New York: Dover Publications, 1994.

Weir, Alison. *Elizabeth the Queen.* London: Jonathan Cape, 1998.

Weir, Alison. *Henry VIII: The King and His Court.* New York: Ballantine Books, 2001.

Weir, Alison. *Lancaster and York: The Wars of the Roses.* London: Jonathan Cape, 1995.

Wilson, Richard. *Christopher Marlowe.* New York: Longman, 1999.

WEBSITES

World history site
www.historyworld.net

BBC Online: History
www.bbc.co.uk/history

The Webmuseum's tour of the Renaissance
www.oir.ucf.edu/wm/paint/glo/renaissance/

Virtual time travel tour of the Renaissance
library.thinkquest.org/3588/Renaissance/

The Renaissance
www.learner.org/exhibits/renaissance

National Gallery of Art—tour of 16th-century Italian paintings
www.nga.gov/collection/gallery/ita16.htm

Uffizi Art Gallery, Florence
musa.uffizi.firenze.it/welcomeE.html

Database of Renaissance artists
www.artcyclopedia.com/index.html

Set Index

MAPS
The maps in this book show the locations of cities, states, and empires of the Renaissance period. However, for the sake of clarity, present-day place names are often used.